Book Overview

Unleashing the Divine takes a fresh look at concepts of faith central to a vibrant Christian experience. These include The Mystery, Life, the Spirit, the Church, the Kingdom, and others. These concepts have suffered years of trite use, cultural attack, and shallow interpretation thus sapping the vitality of Christian faith in America. These words are sung, prayed and used everyday without deep meaning. As a result their ability to bring believers to a mature faith has been weakened. The book recaptures the depths of these concepts encouraging committed believers and energizing those whose faith has become legalistic or boring. It kindles a passion for Christ and a desire to pursue him with others of similar passion. Though the power of these concepts has been lost to many, there is hope. This book presents practical suggestions to restore that hope in language that is simple yet profound. Believers from 18 to 80 will find encouragement in its pages.

Author Profile

Lance Thollander is President of Hope Builders International, a Christian organization serving missions endeavors worldwide. He holds an MA in Education and has spent 20 years in education and 13 years in missions work. Since coming to Christ in the late 60's he has had a passion to see the Lord exalted and the church of Christ expressed in fullness living under Jesus' headship.

b

Unleashing the Divine: Recapturing our Christian Vocabulary

Lance Thollander

Published in Afton, Virginia by Forge Life Press

Forge Life Press is a division of

Hope Builders International
PO Box 317
Greenwood, VA 22943
540-456-7300

Unless otherwise identified, all Scripture quotations in this
publication are taken from the New American Standard Bible
(NASB), © The Lockman Foundation 1960, 1962, 1963, 1968, 1971,
1972, 1973, 1975, 1977.

Additional copies can be ordered at the above address or online at:

www.forgelifepress.com

ISBN: 0-9790019-0-0

Printed in the United States of America

To Christie

We have shared this adventure for thirty-five years. The experience described herein is yours as much as it is mine. Here's to the greater adventures that lie ahead as we follow on after the Lord Jesus. I love you deeply.

f

Acknowledgements

This book was made possible through the contributions of many friends and loved ones. I particularly wish to thank my wife and co-worker Christie and children, Joel, his wife Louisa, Jon, Matt and Jennie, who provided much valuable input into the content. You all are the joy of my life. The encouragement, editing advice and discerning comments of Mark Haskins were of inestimable value in the manuscript's development and publishing process. Without his help the book would likely not have come together. I am grateful to my co-workers Johan and Lida Gous, Peter and Hanri Kaya, Alexis Crow and Dana Andrechyn, for their hearts of love for the Lord Jesus and supporting me in this endeavor. The Board of Directors of Hope Builders International, Tom Mohn, Rick Cain, Raleigh Althisar and Mark Haskins pushed me for two years to get this project done and have been nothing but enthusiastic about the result. Others including Bob Emery, Ann Witkower, Ken Jones, Katie Porsch and Charles and Nor Thollander provided helpful insight into the book's content and layout. I am grateful to Alee Thollander who did a beautiful job of capturing the book's essence in the front and back cover designs. I also wish to thank Gene Edwards for building in my life a foundation of love for Jesus Christ, and giving a young group of Christians many years ago the freedom to follow the Lord Jesus into heavenly realms. Those realms await us all.

h

Chapters

Unleashing the Divine:

Recapturing our Christian Vocabulary

Introduction

Words have tremendous power. When used effectively they have the ability to sway nations, captivate hearts, stir warriors to great valor and take us on journeys of deep and lasting emotion. This is God's design.

Indeed, God called his son Jesus, the greatest force for change in all history, The Word. In short, words have the power to change us. From the beginning God had in mind a deep communication with his beloved creation, a communication so intimate that its end result would be the dispensing of God himself, through Christ, into you and me.

To that end throughout Scripture, the Lord introduces us to wondrous words, full of meaning and carrying an invitation to realms of experience found only in the depths of God himself; words like Life; the Kingdom; the heavens; the Word of God; the Mystery; the Church; and the Spirit. These profound words were designed to change us. But do they?

It is my contention that the power these words have to show us the way to intimate fellowship with God has largely been lost. They have become so commonplace in our Christian vocabulary that we assume we have plumbed their depths. We sing them, pray them, and use them every day without taking the time to explore them.

For us to gain a deep understanding of these words is a threat to God's enemy, because of their power to invigorate our communication with God. God's enemy has a fixed interest in stripping that power away. In fact there is an unrelenting tendency for the precious storehouse of our Christian vocabulary to be watered down and ultimately stripped of its deep meaning by our culture, by our enemy and even by the religious establishment itself. The fact is that as our precious God-spoken words are co-opted by the world around us, the realm of experience they represent becomes nothing more than a faint memory or a distant hope.

American Christianity has sometimes been described as "a mile wide and an inch deep." One survey taken by the Barna Group reported that 85% of American Christian men find attending church to be spiritually unchallenging. They are bored by what they encounter there. Is that the case with you? If so, could this decline in spiritual vitality be related to the meaninglessness of many of the words that should convey the joy and adventure of our Christian journey?

Most definitely!!

It's high time to set the record straight.

Take, for example, the word "life." How basic could a word be? But what type of life does the New Testament present to us? How does the life you are experiencing now relate to the life you will experience in the ages to come? And what exactly did Jesus mean when he said, "*As the living Father sent me and I live by the Father, he who eats me, shall live by me?*" These are profound questions.

How about the word "mystery"? What was so amazing about the mystery that Paul would base his ministry on it and want to be remembered mainly as a "steward of the mystery"? (I Corinthians 4:1) Then there's the message of the kingdom. What was so intensely practical about this kingdom that Paul first spent two years in Ephesus and then two more years in Rome preaching about it? What would it be like to hear two years' worth of glorious ministry on the kingdom of God? That sounds like a journey of discovery worth embarking on. Are you ready to go?

Part of our inheritance as Christians is to fully comprehend these words that can fill us with passion, joy and longing for our God. My aim in writing this book is to challenge seeking believers to explore and then reclaim the deep meaning and experience of these words to such an extent that when we hear them, we can't help but exclaim, "How sweet the sound!"

This book will direct you back to the richness of your Christian vocabulary; to take back what is rightfully yours. But be forewarned! We are not after just the words themselves, but the experiences that these words make available to us. This journey requires a believing heart. You will be challenged to rethink how these words have been handled as we examine the misrepresentations that have sought to diminish these treasures. You will find that much too often these words have been used to fortify petty Christian squabbling rather than used to find the gateway into deep fellowship with our God.

Realize as well that ultimately this journey will require friends. You will discover that these words lead you into a realm where God is most fully known in the fellowship of his people. They were not designed for use in an individual pursuit of God where all is dependent on a lone believer finding the keys to living "the abundant Christian life."

As the meaning and truth of these words are uncovered and the depths of what God has given us are seen, your heart will be stirred. This is a journey into God's own thoughts, a journey that leads to a lifetime of discovery as God takes us deeper and deeper into the glorious mystery that is his son, Jesus Christ.

The journey begins with a willingness to examine these familiar, oft-passed over, culturally trivialized and under-appreciated words and to replace your understanding of them with a higher vision. There's little to lose. With an estimated three American churches closing down every day and counterfeit religions advancing across our nation, Americans need a new encounter with the living

Christ and his people. It starts with what we believe about who God is and the words he uses to communicate his purpose to us.

Are you ready to do some recovery work? Then let's get to it!

Lance Thollander
Afton, Virginia

The Mystery

"But we speak God's wisdom in a mystery" **1 Corinthians 2:7**

Do you like a good mystery? Do you enjoy being in on a big secret? Most people do. There is actually something in our hearts that is intrigued by the mysterious. We are drawn to it. In its pure form that sense of the mysterious was put there by God, himself.

Every mystery includes a secret, something hidden that keeps the mystery from being openly known. Until we know that secret, we cannot fully solve the mystery.

Many believers are not aware that God had a secret. It was the best kept secret of all time and we are part of it. Yes, you and I were created as part of the greatest mystery the world has ever known. In the most real way, we are part of the revealing of this mystery. In fact, uncovering the riches of this mystery is a vital element on our journey to recapturing our Christian vocabulary. In the process, the divine activity of the Lord will be unleashed in our walk with him.

The Bible in its essence is a mystery book. The Scriptures contain the deep secrets of God. They can bring us deeper into adventure with him than we could have ever imagined. But Christians often treat God's mystery as a doctrine to be learned or a truth to be picked up; simply one teaching among many in our journey through the Bible. Few are awed by this mystery. Few are driven by its deep meaning as was the apostle Paul. Few are

7

encouraged to plumb the depths of the secret that God wove into creation.

Jesus Christ referred to the mystery early in his ministry. He said to his followers, *"Unto you it is given to know the mysteries of the kingdom of God: but unto them that are without, all these things are done in parables"* (Mark 4:11). There is a mysterious element in God's kingdom. The Lord desires to unlock the secret of that mystery for those who follow him.

Paul referred to the mystery when he wrote in 1 Corinthians 2:6-10, *"But we speak wisdom among those who are mature, a wisdom however not of this age, nor of the rulers of this age who are passing away; but we speak God's wisdom in a mystery, the hidden wisdom, which God predestined before the ages to our glory, which none of the rulers of this age understood, for if they had understood it, they would not have crucified the Lord of glory."*

There is much to be gleaned from this amazing passage. It confirms the fact that there was a mystery hidden in God as he began to create. Amazingly enough, the fulfillment of this mystery results in our glory. The Westminster Confession, the foundational document of Presbyterian faith, says that the chief end of man is to glorify and enjoy God. That is true, but according to Paul's words above, the mystery involves us being made glorious! At the end of time, God will receive glory, but we also will be glorified. How that will be accomplished is at the heart of the mystery.

The Mystery and the Rulers of this Age

I Corinthians tells us that there are rulers of this age that do not understand this mystery. Who are the rulers of this age? Consider these passages from Paul:

Ephesians 3:10: *"...so that the manifold wisdom of God might now be made known through the church to the rulers and authorities in the heavenlies."* Ephesians 6:12: *"For we wrestle not against flesh and blood, but against the rulers, against the powers, against the world forces of this darkness, against spiritual forces of wickedness in the heavenlies."* Colossians 2:15: *"When he [God] had disarmed the rulers and authorities, he made a public display of them having triumphed over them through him [Christ]."*

These passages refer to those beings who rule in heavenly places. There is no doubt that the earthly rulers who were in power in the first century did not comprehend the mystery of who Jesus Christ was. But in the bigger picture of God's eternal purpose, Paul was referring here to the spiritual powers, principalities and rulers who were behind those earthly powers. Their ruler, Satan himself, said to Jesus regarding the kingdoms of this world, *"All these will I give you, if you will fall down and worship me"* (Matthew 4:9). Satan is the present ruler of this age and, as such, his failure to comprehend God's mystery will result in his ultimate destruction.

The point to remember is that before time began, before there was an earth, a sun, a moon or stars, God had a wonderful, wise and mysterious plan. Before there were rivers, lakes, horses, birds or bushes, God had a secret. Paul said that this mystery, this secret, was so important to God's plan that if the rulers of the age had understood it, they would not have crucified their arch enemy, the Lord of glory. That's how powerful this mystery is.

Paul goes on to say: *"...things which eye has not seen, and ear has not heard, which have not entered the heart of man, all that God has prepared for those who love him. For to us God revealed them through the Spirit: for the Spirit searches all things, even the depths of God"* (I Cor. 2:9-10).

Whatever we can imagine of the great things that God has in store for us does not come close to the reality of what God has planned. Praise God! But there is a way that we can gain understanding regarding this age-old secret. That understanding comes through the revelation of his indwelling Spirit. We can understand what the rulers of darkness could not.

The Mystery Takes Revelation

Paul elaborated on this mystery when he wrote to the church in Ephesus: *"...he made known to us the mystery of his will, according to his kind intention which he purposed in Christ, with a view to a fellowship suitable to the fullness of the times, the summing up of all things in Christ, things in the heavens and things on earth"* (Ephesians 1:9).

God the Father had a secret in mind when he created the earth. God the Son embodied that mystery when he was sent in human form. God the Spirit revealed that secret to the apostle Paul so that Paul could make it known throughout the world. That mystery includes the gathering together, the summing up of all things in Jesus Christ. Whatever is in the heavens, whatever is on the earth is going to be headed up by Jesus Christ.

The servant Christ, the One who laid down his life as a lamb, becomes the leader, the head, and the chief executive of all things in this universe. The governing of all things will rest on his gracious shoulders. That will come as a surprise to most people who have lived on this planet. But Paul was not done explaining. Here's what he wrote later in the same letter: *"By revelation there was made known to me the mystery; as I wrote before in brief. By referring to this you can understand my insight into the mystery of Christ, which in other ages was not made known to the sons of men, as it is now revealed to his holy apostles and prophets in the Spirit; that the Gentiles are fellow heirs, and fellow members of the body and fellow partakers of the promise in Christ Jesus through the gospel.... [T]o me, the very least of all saints, this grace was given, to preach to the Gentiles the unfathomable riches of Christ; and to bring to light what is the fellowship of the mystery, which for ages has been hidden in God, who created all things so that the manifold wisdom of God might now be made known by the church to the rulers and authorities in heavenly places"* (Ephesians 3:3-10).

Here Paul expanded on what the mystery included. The secret is directly connected to Jesus Christ and to his body, the church. The church here is not a building on a downtown corner. The church is all those whom God has called out of the jurisdiction of his enemy and brought into the kingdom of light. The riches of Christ are to be shared in fellowship with those called-out ones and made known by them to the rulers and authorities. That's a marvelous plan.

Paul says that it takes a revelation from God to understand the mystery. But what does it mean to have a revelation? Does it mean we see something about angels and rushing winds and giant horsemen?

Not in this case.

Revelation is God simply allowing us to know with our hearts what's real. To reveal something is to show what's there, to pull back the curtain and show what's going on behind the scenes. God wants us to understand what his great eternal secret is so that we can be part of its revealing. For thousands of years God held on to this secret, waiting for the day when he would reveal it. Think how hard it is to keep a secret for ten minutes, let alone an hour, or a day, or a year. But God held on to the greatest secret ever known until the fullness of time came. That time began with the physical, yet divine birth of Jesus some two thousand years ago.

God wanted the disciples to understand the mysteries of his kingdom. He wanted Paul to understand the secret of his great plan. Now he wants you and me to understand it as well. Notice the emphasis on the words "fellow" and "fellowship" in the passage above. The Gentiles, those who were not originally part of God's chosen people, Israel, were to be fully part of God's people—fellow members of God's family, fellow heirs of God's riches and fellow partakers of the promised Christ. These Gentile nations who were considered unclean and hated by the nation of Israel were to become fully one with Jewish believers in the inheritance that God had for his people. Not only that, those nations who were far away from God and without hope in the world were invited to join in the intimate fellowship of the Father and the Son. This was revolutionary!

The Mystery Involves Fellowship

This mystery involves fellowship at the deepest level between our Lord and those who put their faith in him. Through that fellowship God shares his incredible and multi-faceted wisdom with his body, his church. That's us! We, in turn, make that wisdom known to the rulers and principalities in heavenly places. What an important part we have to play!

Will God's plan work? Did God know what he was doing in redeeming fallen humans and placing his greatest treasure in them? Eternity will show the answer to be a resounding Yes!

But there's more to learn from Paul on this subject.

In Colossians 1:25-27 we read this: *"I was made a minister according to the stewardship from God bestowed on me for your benefit that I might fully carry out the word of God, the mystery, which has been hidden from the ages and generations but has now been manifested to his saints, to whom God willed to make known what is the riches of the glory of this mystery among the nations, which is Christ in you, the hope of glory."*

The saints Paul was talking about here are simply those who had truly believed in Christ. They are the ones God makes holy by cleansing them with the blood of his Son. To Paul, fully carrying out the word of God included revealing the mystery that Christ, in all his glory, would come to live in his saints (that's us believers). Going farther, through us he would make his glory known to the nations. That means we are a part of the fullness of God, made to enjoy and show forth the riches of Christ for all eternity. What a hope!

Paul hammered the point home in the first few verses of Colossians 2: *"For I want you to know how great a struggle I had on your behalf...that your hearts may be encouraged, having been knit together in love... as you fully come to understand God's mystery, Christ, in whom are hidden all the treasures of wisdom and knowledge."*

Let's review. Before time began, God had a mystery, a secret which he hid within himself. The mystery would result in our glory and involved both Jew and Gentile. This mystery finds fulfillment through Christ living in us. And this mystery is so important, so earth shattering, that if the rulers of this age had understood it (and they did not understand it), they would not have crucified the Lord Jesus Christ.

So what is the mystery? Clearly we can all repeat Paul's words that the mystery is Christ in us. But if we say that and then simply go on to the next truth or the next sermon or the next Christian activity, we have not plumbed its depths. Paul was captivated and motivated by this mystery. This was not something that he learned about in his first six months of being a Christian and then filed away in his memory bank so he could move on to other things. He was called by God to go out and carry the message of this mystery to the nations. He asked the churches of Asia to pray for him that he would boldly proclaim it. He told the Corinthians that he wished to be regarded as its steward. Even in his enduring words to the Ephesians about the intimacy of marriage, he could not help but say that the reality of this deep relationship was really wrapped up in the mystery of Christ living in union with his people.

If the mystery is so central, then, how can we better understand it?

The Mystery and Creation

Let's go back and consider creation. By watching how God worked in Genesis 1 we find clues that enlighten us. God created the heavens and the earth. Then he introduced light and separated light from darkness. Next he began to build on the visible creation.

As God built, consider his pattern: *"And God said, Let the earth bring forth grass,* **herbs yielding seed**, *and fruit trees yielding fruit* **after their kind, with seed in it,** *upon the earth: and it was so....And the earth brought forth grass, and* **herb yielding seed after its kind**, *and the tree yielding fruit,* **with seed in it, after its kind**: *and God saw that it was good....And God said, Let the waters bring forth abundantly the moving creature that hath life, and fowl that fly above the earth....And God created great whales, and every living creature that moves, which the waters brought forth abundantly,* **after their kind**, *and every winged fowl* **after its kind**: *and God saw that it was good....And God said, Let the earth bring forth the living creature* **after its kind**, *cattle, and creeping thing, and beast of the earth* **after its kind**: *and it was so. And God made the beast of the earth* **after its kind** *and cattle* **after their kind**, *and every thing that creeps upon the earth* **after its kind**: *and God saw that it was good."*

Do you see the pattern? There is one significant point made over and over again in the Genesis account. Everything that God created had a common characteristic. Everything contained seed. And, in the most natural of ways, that seed produced its own kind.

That simple fact is tremendously significant. The grass, the bushes, the trees, animals, birds, and beasts—everything produced its own kind. Apples have seed in them that produces more apples. Oranges have seed in them that produces oranges. Monkeys produce monkeys and kangaroos produce kangaroos. This is not rocket science, but it tells us something profound about God's plan for this universe. Remember, in all of this, God had a secret.

Behind the universe that God created was a mystery. But as he created, God left clues as to what that mystery was. God's creation calls out to us every day declaring the simplicity of this mystery. When you see magnificent oak trees, you might be impressed by their grandeur. You may love sitting in their shade. But in the fall of the year, when you look at the ground under them, you see thousands of acorns, all carrying the potential of future grand oaks inside of them. They are all hinting at this mystery. All those oak seeds are trying to tell us the secret. "I came from an oak tree, I will be an oak tree and one day, I will produce oak trees."

Thanks for the science lesson, but what does it have to do with me?

Plenty.

There was one significant departure from the creation pattern that makes all this dynamically relevant. Grass produces after its kind, oranges bear the image of oranges, birds produce more birds, cattle look and sound like the cattle that came before them. But look what happened when it came to the creation of man:

Genesis 1:26-27: *"And God said, Let us make man* **in our image, after our likeness***: and let them have dominion over the fish of the sea, and over the fowl of the air, and over the cattle, and over all the earth, and over every creeping thing that creeps upon the earth… so God created man* **in his own image, in the image of God created he him; male and female created he them.** *"*

Who is man supposed to look like? What image was man supposed to bear?

Man was to bear the image of God!

That's amazing. The human community, made up of men and women contributing equally, was not to bear the image of man. Men and women, God's highest creation, were to bear God's image and to represent God's likeness on this planet. But that didn't happen. The rulers and the principalities in heavenly places looked down and saw the man that God had created. They saw that this man was given dominion over the earth—earth they considered to be their territory. So, Satan, through the instrument of a serpent, invaded the Garden. He deceived Adam and Eve, and they were tarnished by sin. They lost their dominion over the earth and the possibility of bearing the image of God.

That is why, when you look at humanity around the world today and the civilizations that mankind has produced, you do not see the glory of God. You do not see the image of a glorious, creative, loving and mighty God. Instead you see the image of a fallen humanity and the forces of darkness who have taken jurisdiction over the planet. That's why the enemy said to Jesus Christ in the wilderness that all the kingdoms of the world would be his if Jesus would worship the evil one.

The rulers thought that in deceiving Adam they had destroyed God's plan. They knew the man had become sinful and had lost the ability to bear the image of a holy God. But they made a miscalculation, because they did not know about God's mysterious plan. God's dream would not be thwarted!

God started working anew, through the Israelites. He drew near to them through the law, the priesthood, the tabernacle and the temple. But all those things only pictured what God really wanted. All of those things were copies of something heavenly that God revealed to Moses on Mount Sinai. God had a secret, not yet ready for revealing.

The Mystery Unfolds in Real Time

Finally, the fullness of time came. Jesus Christ was born in human flesh. Read what John had to say about him starting in John 1:14: *"The Word became flesh and dwelt among us and we saw his glory, glory as of the only begotten of the Father, full of grace and truth....For the law was given through Moses; grace and truth were made real in Jesus Christ. No one has seen God at any time, the only begotten God who is in the bosom of the Father, he has explained him."*

At last the one who truly bore the image of God had come to earth. At last all could look and see what God was really like. This

One had dominion over the creeping things. He had dominion over the powers of darkness. He could teach like no one before him. He could turn water into wine and a small lunch into a meal for thousands. He was, in fact, the man Adam was modeled after back in Genesis.

But do we find in any one of those attributes the whole secret? Was the secret that Jesus Christ came to be a great teacher? Did he come primarily to be a great healer? Or was his secret that he was a miracle worker? Or perhaps that he came to be king?

In John, chapter 2, Jesus went to a wedding. When the hosts ran out of wine, his mother came to tell him about the problem. He replied, *"My time has not yet come."* In John 7 his brothers wanted him to go up to the feast and make a public statement. Again he responded, *"My time has not yet come."* Jesus had come to this planet with a specific purpose and timetable in mind. He spoke with authority, he revealed the glory of God, he healed, and he raised people from the dead. His followers wanted to make him king. As wonderful as all those things are, the unveiling of Christ as teacher, prophet, healer, miracle worker and earthly king did not fully reveal the mystery of his great purpose.

His enemies thought they did. The prince of darkness, the principalities and rulers of this age and those Pharisees who feared him saw in Jesus a man on the earth they couldn't control. He was the one person on earth over whom they did not have dominion. The enemy was in control of the entire planet, so he led Jesus Christ up to a high mountain. He promised Jesus all the kingdoms of earth if Jesus would submit to him. He would give the kingdoms to Jesus if only Jesus would bow down and worship him. But God's enemy was and is a liar. He had no intention of turning anything over to the Lord Jesus.

Here was a man the enemy could not control or deceive. Such an offer might have swayed the rest of mankind, but it did not sway the Lord Jesus. His reply has rung through the ages: *"You shall worship the Lord your God and serve him only."* Truly, Jesus Christ was a different type of man, a new man. He lived by a life that was divine, the life of God that was in him. As he walked on earth, he revealed the true nature of God to those who had eyes to see. The people wanted to make him King. But Jesus was not looking for an earthly kingdom. God had something greater in mind—something that involves you.

Though the people longed for Jesus to step forward and take control, he refused. His hour had not yet come—the hour when all would be revealed; the hour when God's secret would be displayed. Finally, after three years of revealing God to mankind, Jesus headed for Jerusalem for the great feast of the Passover. Tension filled the air. His followers hailed him as King. His enemies plotted his death.

The Nations are Added

Events were drawing to a climax. The crucifixion of the Lord Jesus was drawing near. John described what happened next: *"Now there were some Greeks among those that were going up to worship at the feast: these then came to Philip and asked him, saying, Sir, we wish to see Jesus. Philip came and told Andrew, Andrew and Philip came and told Jesus. And Jesus answered them, saying, 'The hour has come for the Son of man to be glorified. Truly, truly, I say unto you, except a grain of wheat fall into the ground and dies, it abides alone: but if it dies, it brings forth much fruit. He that loves his life shall lose it; and he that hates his life in this world shall keep it unto life eternal'"* (John 12:20-25).

Jesus Christ was about to be crucified. The time of his physical presence on earth was about to end. Up to this point Jesus brought his message to God's chosen people, the Israelites. But then the disciples were approached by non-Jews who want to see Jesus, to follow Jesus.

The apostles looked at each other. They weren't sure if that was allowed. They thought the gospel was for them, the chosen people of Israel. Now these outsiders who had no claim to Jesus wanted to see him. The two went to Jesus and told him, "Some from the non-Jewish world are here to see you." As he heard the news, Jesus made this incredible statement: *"Now, my hour has come."* The Jews knew who he was. Now those from the non-Jewish nations were coming in. The stage was set. Whatever reason the Lord had come for was about to be revealed.

Jesus Christ declared, *"Unless a grain of wheat falls into the ground and dies, it abides alone. But if it dies, it bears much fruit."* The Lord finally pulled back the curtain. He was a grain of wheat, a seed that would go into the ground and die. Then, rising again, he would produce the fruit of his life in those who would follow him! Jesus Christ is the reality of all that seed that we read about in Genesis 1. He is the seed of God who would produce the image of God in his people. He is the one who would make possible and real God's words, "Let us make man in our image, after our likeness." That was and is the work of Christ. He is bringing it to pass!

The Mystery Revealed

Finally we come to the heart of the mystery. Finally we come to the secret for which Christ came to earth. He came to be a seed. He came to fall into the ground and die. Then, through his resurrection he would produce much fruit for God.

How was Jesus going to produce that fruit? He would do it as the Holy Spirit. As Spirit, Jesus Christ would be able to indwell his people. Through the power of his life in them, they could bear his image. They could show to the rulers and authorities the manifold wisdom of God.

Think back to what happened after the crucifixion. Jesus Christ had died. His disciples were gathered in an upper room, not knowing what to do next. The Lord they loved was gone. Then, miraculously, he walked through a closed and locked door into their midst. The chaos of mass jubilation ensued. Then Jesus said this: *"Peace is with you: as the Father has sent me, I also send you."* When he had said this, he breathed on them, and said, *"Receive the Holy Spirit."*

Through his death and resurrection Jesus Christ became the life-giving Spirit. As the Spirit, he could indwell those who believed in him. The Jews had been invited. Now the nations were coming to seek Christ. Now God revealed his secret plan to put Christ into all who wanted to know him. Christ, the living seed, would produce the image of God in them. As one body, these believers would express the life of God on the earth. Not only that, in the ages to come they will dwell together, exploring the unfathomable riches that are in Jesus Christ. This is the mystery revealed.

Look around! Every orange that you eat bears witness to the mystery. Every sunflower loaded with seed gives testimony to God's secret. Christ, the seed of life, Christ, the image and fullness of God, is now available to all. Christ went into the ground to die so that he could get his life into us and fill us with himself. That is the mystery that propelled Paul.

If the rulers of this age had understood the mystery, they would not have crucified the Lord of Glory. Why not? When Jesus Christ walked the dusty roads of Israel, teaching, healing and working miracles, Satan knew that a power greater than he was loose on this planet. His dominions knew that a higher authority had arrived. But they also knew they had everything else under their control. They thought that if they could just get rid of this Jesus, everything would be back to normal. Jesus could only be in one place at a time, whether it was in Cana turning water into wine, in Bethany raising Lazarus, or in Jerusalem proclaiming that a new kingdom was coming. His range was limited. If he could just be killed, then the rulers would be back in control. They thought they had taken care of Christ on the cross.

But God had a secret.

The Mystery and You

Jesus Christ was crucified and placed into the ground. The enemy thought the problem of Jesus had finally, permanently, been dealt with. But there was one thing those rulers did not understand: The life that was in Christ was greater than all the forces of death and darkness combined. They did not know that Jesus Christ would come bursting out of that grave. They had no idea that he would ascend to his Father and be wondrously glorified. They had no clue that he was going to return to earth and breathe his spirit life into his disciples.

God's plan from the beginning of time was revealed. The people of God, through Christ living in them, would now show forth the image of God. As God's people, known as the church, functioned together as a body, sharing the riches of Christ in them, the image and rule of God would be expressed over this whole planet.

The forces of darkness thought they had quenched the source of light and life.

Far from it! Now the light spread.

No longer was Jesus confined to one physical location. No longer was Satan opposed simply in one town in Galilee.

The rulers and principalities don't just have trouble in Jerusalem anymore. They have trouble in Charlottesville, Virginia, in Nepal, in India, in Turkey, across the continent of Africa and wherever you live. Why? Because Jesus Christ lives today wherever his church is found. Wherever his people live under his headship, souls are brought out of darkness, people are saved from lives of meaningless despair and the power of the enemy is broken. The expansion of light, life and love follow in their train.

If Christ, the seed of Life, is in you, you are part of the revealing of the greatest secret in time and eternity. If not, why not stop now and invite the living Christ to make his home in you through his Holy Spirit? This is the purpose for which you were created.

The mystery is revealed as we know Christ and become transformed by his life. The greatest gift we can give new believers is to share this revelation with them. The living Christ, through the Holy Spirit, has actually come to live in them. So begins the greatest adventure we can know in time and eternity. But receiving Christ is only the beginning. The Lord Jesus comes into us as a seed and patiently works his life into us. Knowing Christ, sharing Christ and learning how to live in unity with other believers is God's desire for us. In the ages to come we will be occupied with this same great endeavor, plumbing the depths, the length, the width and the height of the unfathomable riches of Jesus Christ.

This is why Paul told the Corinthians he wanted to be regarded as a steward of the mystery. What greater honor could there be? May God give us ever increasing revelation regarding the greatness of his mystery, Christ in us, the hope of glory.

Life

"I am come that they might have life..." John 10:10

"Dad, what's it all about? Why are we here?" my 16-year-old son suddenly asked as we drove down a Sacramento street a number of years ago.

I caught my breath. How do you come up with an instant answer to the eternal question of the universe, especially one that will make sense to a teenager?

The answer to that simple, yet profound, question is tied directly to a simple, yet profound, word: life. God's plan for us involves life.

Most believers in Christ are very familiar with the passage cited above. Jesus tells his followers that he has come that we might have life and have it in abundance. John reinforced this same point when he wrote, *"Therefore many other signs Jesus also performed in the presence of the disciples, which are not written in this book; but these have been written so that you may believe that Jesus is the Christ, the Son of God; and that believing you may have life in his name"* (John 20:30-31).

God clearly wants to give us life.

If we are not careful, however, we can easily overlook the tremendous depth of this truth. Or, worse still, its meaning can be trivialized in our experience or relegated to a distant time of future importance. Too many believers in Christ think of the life referred to in John 10 as simply a quality of life. We may think of the Christian life as a happy life, a life where our sins are forgiven, our basic needs are met, God is on our side and we are on our way to live forever in heaven. You may have heard this described as "the abundant Christian life."

What about the Abundant Christian Life?

These concepts are not bad. But if your goal is simply to live an outwardly successful Christian life, you will not experience on this planet the fullness that God has in mind for you. You were created for more.

In your efforts to have the "abundant life," you may have worked hard to build a happy and seemingly secure life. But you still find yourself somehow unfulfilled. There are times when Bible reading becomes a chore; church attendance becomes routine; your relationship with Christ becomes distant; your relationships remain shallow.

In addition, life has dealt you some major setbacks. Even though you earnestly want to follow Christ, you experience disappointment and disillusionment with your walk with him and your experience with other believers. Your response may be to feel defeated, to think that you have somehow let the Lord down or that he has let you down. If you can relate to any of the above, take heart. There is a richer experience of Christ available.

The fact is that the life God wishes us to have is far different than outwardly looking successful. It's time to restore the deeper meaning and experience inherent in the word "life." The Gospel of John reveals what God has in mind. John 1:4 tells us that Jesus Christ was unique in the entire universe when it says, *"In him was life and the life was the light of men."*

Jesus Had Divine Life

While we may rightly assume that everyone has life, John was talking about a totally different kind of life.

John was referring here to divine life, the life of God himself. There was a type of life in Jesus that was different than the life that was in anybody else. In Christ was the divine, supernatural, spirit life of God the Father. In the light that emanated from that life, the darkness of all mankind became evident.

Consider John 3:16, the best-known Bible verse in the world: *"For God so loved the world that he gave his only begotten son, that whoever believed in him should not perish but have eternal life."* When it comes to this verse, too often we think, "Okay, that means I believe in Jesus, and when I die, I'm going to go to heaven where I'm going to live forever in a big mansion on a street of gold." While that may be the perspective of many, God was thinking in a different direction.

What the Lord was talking about here is the life that was in him, the type of life that he had. Jesus walked on planet earth exhibiting heavenly behavior because in him there was a heavenly kind of life. It's divine life. The Scriptures tell us in John 3:13 that *"As Moses lifted up the serpent in the wilderness, so must the Son of Man be lifted up, that whoever believes may, in him, have eternal life."* Whoever believes in the Son is going to get that heavenly life that he has.

Where is Life?

Now let's consider where this life is kept. John 5:26 says this: *"the Father has life in himself."* Make a note: the Father had life **in himself**, *"So he gave to the Son to have life…**in himself**."* Make another note: the Son, Jesus Christ, had life in himself. And now, through the death and resurrection of Jesus Christ, in one of the most significant developments of human history, when we receive Jesus Christ, we have that life **in** ourselves. Yes, it's true. God invites you to have this same life **in yourself** through Christ Jesus.

The end of the passage tells us, *"You search the Scriptures because you think in them you'll have eternal life."* The Pharisees thought, "If I just study the scrolls of the Old Testament, I'll understand the mysteries of life." But the Lord went on, *"Those bear witness of Me, but you're unwilling to come to Me that you may have Life!"* The Pharisees came to the Old Testament Scriptures thinking that by diligently studying them they would find life. But they were mistaken; so mistaken that when the real life came along, they couldn't recognize him.

There is no book as glorious as the Bible. It stands alone as God's inerrant word to mankind. I depend on it for refreshment, revelation and life. But there are times when the Bible can lose its vitality. Has that happened to you? This may be because it has become to you simply a source of knowledge rather than the book of life.

Let's say you have sought to be a good Christian, diligently reading the Bible and working hard to put what you read into practice. But something has been missing. You have come up short of real life. You are making a noble effort and it seems to work for a while, but over the course of time you keep running out of gas. I know what you are experiencing. I remember as a teenager needing to read through the Bible in order to be confirmed as a church member. It seemed like such an arduous ordeal! I did not experience life. What was wrong?

I was missing Jesus' point, made so long ago. Real life is found in him. Thank God we can touch life through reading the Scriptures. That has never been in dispute. But we do that by linking the Scriptures with the living Christ. The Scriptures are God-breathed, inspired by God himself. So as you come to the Scriptures, allow the living God into your presence. As the Lord meets you, you are going to touch real life.

Life versus Scriptural Correctness

The Pharisees' problem was that they didn't connect the Scriptures with the living Lord who stood before them. And if we fail to connect the Scriptures with the resurrected Christ, we're going to have the same result. This explains why sincere believers can use the Bible to cut each other to pieces. Christians have used the Bible to cause incredible division. How can that be, when we all know that there is value in studying the Scriptures? But you study and find one thing, and someone else studies and finds something else. If the two of you disagree strongly enough, you declare theological war. And you don't quit until everyone in your circles of influence is doctrinally dead. In the process, the unity and life that Christ died and rose again to bring is nowhere to be found. At last count according to the World Christian Encyclopedia there were at least 9000 ways Christians have figured out how to denominate themselves. Can such a statistic please the Lord? Some in each camp may be "right," but "right" isn't the issue.

The issue is life: The Lord said, *"I have come that they might have life."* Instead of life, other things have been elevated: knowledge, doctrine, or emotional experience. Where is the consideration of whether life is produced? If the result of your study doesn't produce life, you need to stop and say, "Lord, have I found you in this?" If it's producing disunity, you need to stop and say, "Hold on! There's something of greater importance and that's finding where real life is."

If I allow my doctrine to separate me from another believer to the extent that we cannot talk nor have fellowship, indeed to the point where we harbor animosity toward one another or look down on one another, then I've settled for something less than life. We are not speaking here about core issues of the Christian faith such as redemption, forgiveness of sin, the resurrection of the Lord Jesus, the indwelling of the Holy Spirit and the inerrancy of the Scriptures that separate us from non-believers. No, we are addressing things that have separated believers from one another, such as church organization, varying beliefs on baptism, the gifts of the Spirit, whether believers can drink wine and on and on.

There is a higher way.

God's Higher Way

Consider Jesus' words in John 10:10: *"The thief comes to kill and destroy, but I have come that they might have... life."* Again, the Lord Jesus makes his purpose plain. *"I have come that they* [that means you and me] *might have Life."*

Is his goal to redeem us? Yes! We need to be redeemed.

Is his goal to cleanse us from sin? Yes, we need to be cleansed from sin.

Is his goal to love us? Yes! And the highest form of his love is to make us part of his own family by sharing with us his life.

What is the best thing that could happen to you? Would it be to receive some great present like a new house or a new car? Such things do not satisfy for long. Or maybe it would simply be to have a problem-free existence. No, there is no such thing. The best thing in this universe is to receive the divine life of God. That's a gift that will stand the test of time and last throughout eternity.

Life: God's Purpose from the Beginning

The purpose of God to give us life was present from the very beginning of creation. Genesis 1:9 says that God made all kinds of trees grow in the Garden of Eden that were pleasing to the eye and good for food. Then he placed two trees in the middle of that garden, the tree of life and the tree of the knowledge of good and evil. In Genesis 2:16, God told Adam that he could eat from any tree in the garden except the tree of knowledge. Eating from that tree would result in his death.

What kind of life was in the tree of life? This tree contained the eternal, divine life of God himself. God, through the tree of life, actually made himself available to the man he had created. But man did not eat of that tree. Indeed, he ate of the very tree that God had warned him not to eat. As a result, man fell. He died spiritually, and God had to close the way to the tree of life, lest man eat from it and live forever in his fallen state. What a disaster that would have been!

But God's purpose to get his life into the man he created would not be thwarted. This same purpose was brought back into focus with the coming of the Lord Jesus in the flesh. He came to share his life with us and re-open the way to the tree of life.

Too often believers think that while their salvation in Christ cannot be earned, following him means working hard at becoming better Christians. That frame of mind leads to a life of comparing yourself to other Christians. But if you receive life and your neighbor receives life, which one of you has more of Christ? Whoever has more is bound to be a better Christian, right?

But there aren't any quantities mentioned. Not one verse in the New Testament talks about having more of Christ. You have life in you if you believe. I have life in me if I believe. Which one of us has more of this life? Neither! Remember, this life is Christ, himself. Therefore, we both have the same access to Christ. You've got him, I've got him. It's not based on how intelligent you are or how much knowledge you have. Nor is it based on your emotions, whether you are feeling good or somewhat down. He can live just as fully in a carpenter or a computer engineer or a single mom as in a theologian or full-time Christian worker. What a great truth!

What then is my prayer? "Lord Jesus, be my life. I volunteer to be a person in whom you live abundantly." Keep in mind that, according to I Peter 1:23, when you receive Christ, you receive him as a seed : *"for you have been born again not of seed which is perishable but imperishable, that is, through the living and enduring word of God."*

A seed is not very big. When you receive new life, the Lord doesn't instantly perfect you, solving all your problems. It may seem that way sometimes in the first blush of your newfound love for the Lord. But as you go on, you discover that living as a Christian is like running an endurance race. Life grows as we grow in our understanding and relationship to Jesus Christ. It will take eternity to fully comprehend all the riches in him.

In John 10:27 and 28, the Lord says this: *"My sheep know me. They hear my voice. And I give to them eternal life."* Can you see that Jesus Christ is on a mission, not to make you a better person, not to insist that you follow the Ten Commandments, not to make you religious, but to actually get himself into you and have you live by him?

God Makes It Practical

But does the Lord make it practical? Knowing that we would need some help in understanding this truth, the Lord presented himself in a form everyone can relate to: food.

In John 6, the Lord feeds five thousand people who have been following him around, listening to him teach. He went away but the people continued to follow him. When they found him the next day, they wanted another free meal. He said, *"Don't work for the food which perishes, work for the food which results in eternal life, which the Son of Man shall give to you."* He made a connection between life and food. There was a food that produced real life. The Lord Jesus was and is that food.

Later in John 6, the Lord literally presented himself as bread. He said, *"**I** am the bread of God, **I** come down out of heaven **to give life to the world.**"* Do you see a pattern here? The Lord Jesus was letting them and us know that he is food and that by eating him we will have real life.

Have you exhausted yourself looking for the key that gives meaning to life? Never-ending ads offer products that promise all we are looking for. But they don't deliver. Maybe you've fasted, taken on a Bible study program, followed a Biblical weight loss regimen, worked extra hours, read a good book on Christian living, or even committed to a special season of prayer, all to find that not much has changed. You might be working too hard. Jesus Christ says, *"I'm the bread of God. If you come to me, you won't hunger. I am here to give life to the world."* He shows us the connection between making him our food and experiencing life.

John 6:57-58 continued to make the point. The Lord said, *"As the living Father sent me and I live by the Father, so he who eats me shall live by me."* What an incredible statement! It sounds so easy. All we have to do is make the Lord our food and we will live by him.

But how do we do that?

One simple starting point is to open your mouth and call on the Lord. Call on his Name throughout the day. Tell him you love him. Fill your mouth with the praises of God. The Scriptures tell us in Psalm 81:10, *"Open your mouth and I will fill it."*

Your relationship with the Lord as life starts in the heart, not the brain. Christ is in you and wants to be your life. Respond to him by inviting him to be your life in the daily decisions that come your way.

A second way to make Christ your food is to spend time in his written Word. Allow the Christ who is in your heart to bring to life the God-breathed words of the Scriptures. Ask the Lord to reveal himself to you in his word and to touch you with his life.

Then begin to read. When you sense his presence, stop and talk to him. Then, let him speak to you. There will come a sense of life, and when you sense that life, you will know it.

A third way to follow the life of Christ within you is to spend time with like-minded believers. Christ is life to believers in every situation, no matter where we find ourselves. But in the big picture, the Lord designed us to be part of his body. To go beyond understanding the real meaning of the word "life" into a rich experience of that life, find some Christian friends who also want to know the Lord as life. We all know it's more enjoyable to share a great meal with friends than to eat one alone. Experiencing Christ is no different.

The Mind Set on the Spirit is Life

Jesus Christ lives in believers through the Holy Spirit. We'll focus on the Spirit in an upcoming chapter, but its helpful now to consider the words of Romans 8:6: *"The mind set on the Spirit is life and peace."* As you learn how to set your mind on the Spirit, you're going to have a sense of life, a sense of peace. The Lord uses that sense to guide you. You may do something that results in your having an internal sense of turmoil. You may say something that results in the same kind of inner distress. It happens. As a result, you'll have an internal sense of heaviness. There won't be a sense of life. There won't be a sense of peace. What do we do in those moments? That's the time to run to the Lord and say, "Lord, You're living in me. I confess that I've made a mistake. There's no life, there's no peace." Ask forgiveness, turn within and find that life and peace. He'll tell you what to do next.

In John 20:31, the apostle John reminded us again, *"The reason I wrote this book is that you might believe and, believing, that* **you might have life in his [Jesus'] Name.** *"* Jesus Christ came, above and beyond everything else, because he wanted to pour his life into you. A renewed understanding of life and the experience contained therein is central to releasing the divine activity of God in us and recapturing our Christian vocabulary.

Your calling is not to remember the Ten Commandments. Your calling is not to try to be a good Christian. Your calling is to fellowship with Jesus Christ as much as possible. He is real life in you, and you are changed by feeding on him.

Life: The Purpose of the Cross

John 17 brings this study of life to a fitting close. The Lord is about to go to the cross. He has gathered his closest friends for final instructions. Surely what is foremost on his heart is going to come out. Here is how the chapter begins: *"These things Jesus spoke and lifting up his eyes to heaven, he said, 'Father, the hour has come; glorify your Son that the Son may glorify you, even as you gave him authority over all mankind, that to all whom you have given him,* **he may give eternal life**. *This is eternal life: that they may know you, the only true God, and Jesus Christ, whom you have sent."*

Jesus couldn't have made it much clearer. The Father gave the Son authority over all mankind, that to all that the Father gave him, **he may give this life**. If you have received this life, you have an open invitation to get to know the Father and the Son in the most intimate of ways. Don't pass it up!

What is eternal life? It's really not that complicated. Eternal life is to know Jesus Christ. Eternal life is to know the Father. Life is not separate from Christ. If you have an experience of life, you've had an experience with the Lord. If you've sensed life in a song or a story shared by a fellow believer or in the Scriptures or in a moment of real need and the Lord has given you peace…if you have had an experience like that, you have had an experience with Jesus Christ.

If you are a believer in Christ, in your spirit right now there is a life that's divine. That life is Jesus Christ, himself. When you turn to him, he is there for you. It's not a thought, it's not an emotion. He is a person who is life.

We must recover the true meaning of this tremendous word, "life." If you will go through the book of John you will see many references to your Lord as life. Once you have seen your Lord as the new life that is in you, you can begin to experience him in new and deeper ways. Will it come easily? No, you can expect a fight. God's enemy will seek to minimize the greatness of your Lord and his power to work in you. But press on! The reward is nothing less than Christ himself.

Heaven, the Realm of God's Presence

"In the beginning, God created the heavens and the earth"

Genesis 1:1

What if I invited you to go to heaven with me?

"Wait," I can hear you saying, "I'm not ready to die yet."

Nonetheless, I invite you to come with me to this most amazing of places. Yes, it will be an eye-opening journey. But be forewarned; when we speak of heaven, we are approaching one of the most misunderstood words in all of our Christian vocabulary.

There are over 700 references to "heaven" in the Bible. This is a place that is very important to God. In the Scriptures the word "heaven" is generally written in the plural and should be translated the heavens or the heavenlies. For example, *"Our Father, who is in heaven"* should be translated, *"Our Father who is in the heavens."* This small distinction is important. It helps us realize that this invisible realm called the heavens is not simply a futuristic place that we are heading for when we die, but it is God's current location, the invisible realm where he is found and where he reigns.

Many different images come to mind when considering the heavenly realm. Some envision it as a place where angels sit around with harps playing soothing music. Others view it as an eternal worship service. Many envision it as a place where large mansions await the faithful and believers stroll down broad golden streets.

Some may even be afraid that an endless life in heaven will be boring,

In reality, the heavens are far more than what these images present. We define heaven as the realm of God's presence, power and authority, a realm created by him for his habitation. God created the heavens as a place where he would dwell and reign and from where he would manage his creation. But the heavens are not just the place where God lives. We, too, have been seated there in the Lord Jesus. Hear Paul in Ephesians 2:6: *"God raised us up with Christ and seated us with him in the heavenly places."* That makes the heavens available to us.

Is Heaven Far Away?

How far away then, are the heavens? As a young boy I remember hearing prayers started out in deep, religious tones, "Our Father who art in heaven," or "Our heavenly Father." These opening words made it seem as though the heavens were millions of miles from where I was. I knew God was in heaven and I hoped he was listening. But he seemed very far away, somewhere above all the stars and the planets.

Though I would never admit it, I wondered how a God who was so far away could really get to where I was. I wondered how he could even hear what I was saying. If you have ever had that impression, take heart. The idea that the heavens are way, way out there is mistaken. Nor is God way out there, either. Such thinking puts a far greater distance between God and his creation than actually exists. "Way out there" is not very accessible. But that's not the case, because God went to great lengths to be totally accessible to us.

Consider how close he was to Jacob in Genesis 28:11-18: *"And Jacob...came to a certain place, and spent the night there; he had a dream and behold a ladder was set on the earth with its top reaching to heaven: and the angels of God were ascending and descending on it; And the LORD stood above it, and said, I am the LORD, the God of Abraham your father, and the God of Isaac: the land on which you lie, I will give it to you and to your descendents.*

Your descendents shall be like the dust of the earth …. and in your descendents shall all the families of the earth be blessed…. Then Jacob awoke from his sleep, and said, surely the LORD is in this place and I didn't know it…how awesome this place is! This is none other than the house of God, and this is the gate of heaven."

Jacob had an amazing experience that night. In his dream the angels of God traveled up and down a ladder that stretched from a stone on earth out into invisible space. God told Jacob that he had a land for Jacob and his descendants. Not only was Jacob to get the land on which he was lying, but out of him would come a blessing for all the nations.

Jacob called that place of interaction between God and man, the house of God, the very gate of heaven. What was going on there? God in heaven was interacting with man on earth. God in heaven was making his will known on the earth. The communication originated in God, but the result was practical blessing on the earth.

From this encounter we can see that the house of God is to be the place where earth and heaven are joined. What does this mean to us? As will be discussed in a future chapter, the present reality of the house of God today is the church…being led by Christ in the heavens. The church was designed to be the vehicle from which God in the heavens would impact the earth. The church was designed to be the gateway between the will of God in heaven and the fulfillment of that will on the earth.

If the house of God is the gate between the heavenly realm and earth, then that realm must be nearer than we think. Many verses in Matthew make the gap between heaven and earth razor thin. In Matthew 3: 2 John the Baptizer said, *"Repent for the kingdom of heaven has come near."*

In chapter 3:16-17 we read, *"After being baptized, Jesus came up immediately from the water: and the heavens were opened and he saw the Spirit of God descending as a dove, and lighting on him And behold a voice out of the heavens said, This is my beloved Son, in whom I am well pleased."*

In chapter 4:17 we read, *"From that time Jesus began to preach, and to say, Repent: for the kingdom of the heavens is at hand."*

Indeed, the kingdom of the heavens was near, so near that what God said in one realm could be heard by humans in the other. In fact, that realm was so near that they were looking right at it. Jesus Christ embodied the kingdom of the heavens!

When Jesus or John spoke of the kingdom of the heavens, they were not speaking about something that was coming two or three thousand years later. When Jesus came to earth he came out of the heavens. Though he was born in Bethlehem, his divine nature was of heavenly origin. He was not coming into friendly territory. John wrote of Jesus: *"In him was life and the life was the light of men, and the light shines in the darkness and the darkness could not overpower it."* Jesus represented a realm that came to assert dominion over an earth in darkness, captured by Satan, the prince of darkness. When God created Adam in Genesis 1, part of Adam's job in the Garden of Eden was to keep the garden, to guard it, to have dominion over it and to rule from it. But Adam failed in his task, and man forfeited the dominion that he was meant to have to Satan and his dominions.

Jesus came to take that rule back, to bring the rule of heaven to earth. He came to usher in the kingdom not with a call to take up arms but with a call to surrender to the living God. This wasn't an earthly kingdom that would rule through force of arms. This kingdom was entirely different. God would rule through his people and be their king.

Jesus Invites Us to Enter Heavenly Realms

Jesus told his followers in Matthew 5:20 that unless their righteousness exceeded that of the Pharisees, they could not enter the kingdom of heaven. This was discouraging news to the twelve. If that were true, entering heaven would be impossible. They looked at the scribes and Pharisees. The disciples observed the religious leaders' priestly outfits, their austere behavior, and their knowledge of the law. From an outward perspective they were impressive.

In our day many have a similar sense when they see a priest, a nun or someone wearing sacramental robes or other religious garb.

Such people are treated with deferential respect simply because of their vestments. The first-century Jews viewed the Scribes and the Pharisees the same way. They were the ones who knew the law, who understood and supposedly practiced what God wanted. They were supposed to be the holy and righteous ones. In the mind of the common man, it wasn't possible to be more righteous than these religious leaders were.

But the Lord knew the Pharisees weren't righteous at all. Not one Pharisee could make it into the kingdom of God on the basis of his good works. The same holds true today for us. Jesus knew there were none righteous. Entrance into the kingdom of heaven was not a matter of obeying the law or being good or putting on an outward show of piety. Entrance into this kingdom is gained through repentance and faith in the One who brought it to earth. He is our access to heavenly realms. He is the ladder which reaches from heaven to earth and back again. Best of all for those first century saints, those listening to Jesus' words would not to have to wait for years to taste the benefits of that heavenly kingdom.

The Lord said that without righteousness, no one could enter the kingdom of the heavens. That is why he went to the cross for our sins; so that God's demand for righteousness could be met. Jesus' expectation is that the heavens, the realm from which his father ruled and made his presence felt, be accessible to those on earth.

Jesus Shows Us the Way

Jesus spoke often of the direct connection between man on earth and God the Father in the heavens. There are over twenty references to that connection in Matthew. Consider these verses from Matthew 6:

Verse 1: *"Beware of practicing your righteousness before men to be noticed by them. Otherwise you have no reward with your Father who is in the heavens."*

Verse 9: *"Pray then, in this way, Our Father who is in the heavens, hallowed is your name. Your kingdom come, your will be done on earth, as it is in the heavens."*

Verse 14: *"For if you forgive men their trespasses, your Father who is in the heavens will also forgive you."*

Verse 26: *"Look at the birds of the air...your Father who is in the heavens feeds them. Are you not much better than they?"*

Verse 32: *"For all these things the Gentiles eagerly seek, for your Father who is in the heavens knows that you need all these things."*

Is it odd that Jesus mentioned five times in the space of five minutes where his Father was? If you heard a speaker do that, you'd likely think he had a problem. But Jesus did not have a problem. He was making the point that he had been sent by his Father out of another realm called the heavens. That realm was where his Father was. Jesus' home base was that realm. By his example Jesus was instructing his followers that, just as he was connected to his Father in the heavens, they, too, would have access to that same realm and that same Father to direct them.

In Matthew 6:6, when the Lord told his followers how to pray, he said, *"But when you pray, go into your inner room and when you have shut your door, pray to your Father who is in secret, and your Father, who sees in secret will repay you."* Where might that secret place be? It must be in heaven because that is God's realm.

When you go into that secret place, God is waiting for you. He wants to reward you with something. And that something is himself. As you fellowship with your Father in heavenly places, he gives you himself. He gives you a sense of peace. He may fill your heart with his love. You may experience a sense of joy in his presence. If you are in despair he may impart the ability to endure in suffering. He could choose to give you a vision of something that is to come. All these are heavenly experiences. Prayer takes us all into the presence of God in his heavenly realm. That's how near this realm is.

Jesus' point is that his Father is in a secret place called heaven. You can go there. This secret place, accessed through your inner being, your spirit, is the place of fellowship for you and your heavenly Father. He is waiting for you there. The apostle Paul backed this up in Ephesians 3:14-16: *"For this reason I bow my knees before the Father from whom every family in heaven and earth derives its name that he would grant you according to the riches of his glory, to be strengthened with power through his Spirit in the inner man."* God builds strength into his people in that secret place. In that secret place you can hear his voice, behold his glory, talk to him, cry out to him, or simply groan before him. Paul referred to that when he wrote in Romans 8:23, *"We ourselves, having the first fruits of the Spirit...groan within ourselves, waiting eagerly for the adoption of sons, the redemption of our bodies."*

The Realm of the Heavens is at Hand.

When the Lord talked about prayer to his followers, he made the relationship between heaven and the rule of God's kingdom clear. Today we, like them, are to pray for his kingdom rule to be made manifest where we live on earth, just as it was when Jesus physically walked on the planet.

God's kingdom was at hand in the person of Christ. Jesus was on earth taking dominion, re-establishing the rule of heaven on earth. His Father's will was being done on the earth as it was in the heavens. A verse in Psalms 115 says, *"God dwells in the heavens, he does whatever he pleases."* Now here was Jesus Christ showing up on earth to take dominion, to re-establish the rule of heaven on earth. That's what he told his disciples to pray. Our prayer should be the same: 'Lord, show us what you're doing in the heavens. Bring your rule to the earth in our lives!"

The Heavens and the Church

In Matthew 16:16-19, Jesus revealed the relationship between the realm of the heavens and the church. These well-known verses read as follows:

"And Simon Peter answered and said, you are the Christ, the Son of the living God. Jesus answered and said unto him, Blessed are you, Simon Barjona: because flesh and blood did not reveal this to you, but my Father who is in the heavens. And I also say to you that you are Peter, and upon this rock I will build my church; and the gates of hell shall not overpower it. I will give to you the keys of the kingdom of heaven: and whatever you bind on earth shall

have been bound in heaven: and whatsoever you shall loose on earth shall have been loosed in heaven."

Here Jesus showed how the church is built and what the role of the church is. Peter testified that Jesus was the Christ, the son of the living God, a revelation he received from God in the heavens. (If Peter had had to wait until the end of time to access the heavenly realm we still wouldn't know how Jesus would build his church.) While some have taken these verses to mean that Jesus would build his church on Peter, a more careful look reveals something greater. Yes, Peter (*petros*, a small stone) would be an important part of the Lord's building. But the church that Jesus was building would be founded on Christ himself. The Greek literally says, *"On this rock, I will build of me the church."* The church will be built out of Christ!

Peter himself made this clear when he wrote many years later, *"And coming to him [Jesus] as to a living stone which has been rejected by men, but is choice and precious in the sight of God, you also, as living stones, are being built up as a spiritual house for a holy priesthood, to offer up spiritual sacrifices acceptable to God through Jesus Christ. For this is contained in Scripture: 'Behold, I lay in Zion a choice stone, a precious corner stone, and he who believes in him will not be disappointed.' This precious value, then, is for you who believe; but for those who disbelieve, 'The stone which the builders rejected, this became the very corner stone'"* (I Peter 2:4-7).

Revelation 21:14 takes the picture a bit farther in showing us how God builds: *"And the wall of the city had twelve foundation stones, and on them were the twelve names of the twelve apostles of the Lamb."* The wall of God's eternal city was built on all the apostles. That tells us that the building of God is a corporate effort. With Christ as the cornerstone, the building goes up among his people. The great news is that not only are the apostles part of that building, we are part of it too!

To facilitate that process the Lord gave to his followers the keys to the kingdom of the heavens. What an amazing statement! The Lord gives his people the keys to unlock the doors to the realm of heaven.

Why?

That's where they will find the material to establish the building. That's where they will find their building instructions. That's where Christ is seated at the right hand of the Father. That's where believers will fellowship with the God who gives real life. The Lord gives to his people the keys to the kingdom of heaven, not the keys to a big vault somewhere loaded with money, or a military base loaded with weapons and ammunition. This is a heavenly kingdom whose presence can be displayed here on earth.

The Lord said that what his people loose on earth will be that which is loosed in heaven; what is bound on earth will be that which is bound in heaven. When he said this, Jesus was explaining what he had been doing and what his disciples would be doing. Christ came to earth to loose the things that his Father had released in heaven. He came to bind the things that the Father had bound in heaven.

He watched what his Father was doing in the heavens and carried that out on the earth. He listened to what his Father was saying and said that on the earth. He loosed and he bound. He set people free and he bound evil spirits. Now, as the body of Christ, that's what we're supposed to do. Jesus implied this when he taught his followers to pray, *"your kingdom come, your will be done, on earth as it is in the heavens."*

The Lord's people are empowered to bind and they're empowered to release. But what are some of the things God wants released? Many think of this in terms of warfare and exercising authority over the powers of darkness. That is certainly a part of the job. But the Lord wants more than that released from his heavenly realm. There are attributes of our loving God that he wants released from this heavenly realm that are needed on a daily basis. Life is one of them. God's people desperately need to see the life of Christ revealed in their midst. Psalms 36 says that God's mercy is in the heavens. We certainly need to see mercy released in our lives and in the lives of those around us. The well-known fruits of the Spirit— love, joy, peace, patience—are all things available to us only in the Lord's heavenly presence. Thank God, we have been given the keys to the realm where they can be experienced.

We all know people who need some joy, some love, or some peace. Maybe they need direction or vision about why they are on this planet. At times we all find ourselves with such needs. These are things that come out of God himself. We have been given access to his kingdom, to heaven itself, and to fellowship with our God. There we receive these things from him and bring them to earth and give them away.

This is what the church is all about. It is God's people together expressing his heavenly will and rule on the earth. Part of that includes binding the enemy from stopping the advance of the gospel. Part of it involves demonstrating the character and image of God that we find in Jesus Christ. In doing these things, the church becomes that which is described in Ephesians 2: "The fullness of him who fills all in all."

This is the reality of what God showed to Jacob when Jacob saw the messengers of God going into and out of the heavens on that heavenly ladder: the people of God going into his presence through Jesus Christ, accessing heavenly realms and reflecting the image of God on the earth.

Our Father's Desire for Us

But there's more. In Matthew 23:9 the Lord said these words: *"Do not call anyone on earth your father, for one is your father, he who is in the heavens."*

What does the Lord mean by these striking words? Let's say you were blessed to have an earthly father who loved you deeply. You owe your presence on this planet to him and your mother. Obviously he would be a very important person in your life. According to Jesus, should you not honor him as such? It must be that the God who instructed his people to "honor their father and mother" was speaking of something deeper.

The Lord was speaking on a spiritual plane. By referring to the way the Jews regarded their religious leaders, he was casting light on our eternal relationship with God. The Jews were not to look to earthly religious leaders as their spiritual fathers, especially those who represented a legalistic way of relating to him. We should exercise the same caution today. We should not bestow lightly a loving title or familial obedience that rightfully belongs to God himself on religious leaders who may or may not know him. It is the God who is in the heavens that has given us spiritual birth. Our true birth is that which originates in him, in heavenly realms.

Our earthly birth enables us to live in the physical environment of this planet. In the same way, our spiritual birth enables us to live in the heavenly air of God's presence. Our God wants us to know that he has given birth to us. We have a right to enter his heavenly presence. As our Father who is in love with us, he wants to exercise the fullness of that love in our lives. That is of eternal significance. For that, God gets all the credit.

There is no question about what Jesus considered to be his real place of origin. Over and over he said, "I am from the heavens." In John 6 he said, *"I am the bread that came down out of the heavens to give life to the world."* Those who followed kept saying: "Why does he say he came out of heaven? Isn't he from Nazareth? Isn't he from Bethlehem?"

Jesus made it clear. He was from the heavens.

Where are you from? Look at the proper translation of Jesus' words in John 3:3: *"Unless a man is born from above, he cannot see the kingdom of the heavens."* If you have been born from above, then you, too, can claim a place in the kingdom of the heavens. We have a right to live on earth because we were born physically here. We have a right to live in the heavens because we were born spiritually in Christ. We access that realm through the Spirit of Christ. Praise God!

Because our Father God has placed his life in us through Christ, we have a legitimate right as a citizen of heaven to go to his realm and fellowship with him. That's why Jesus said not to call any man your father, for you have one Father who is in the heavens. He is waiting for you there and you don't have to wait until you die. That's precious news!

One way to enter his presence is simply to call on the Lord. The Scriptures say that all who call on the Lord will be saved. That means more than just having our sins forgiven. It means the Lord's name has the power to bring us into the presence of our God and save us from the tensions of the world around us. As Proverbs 18:10 tells us, *"The name of the Lord is a strong tower. I will run into it and be safe."* Where is that strong tower? You guessed it: in our Father's heavenly presence.

The Dream Revisited

Let's return to Jacob's vision of the ladder joining earth and heaven and its practical meaning to us today. In John 1:50-51 Jesus shared some information with Nathaniel that Jesus could only know through divine means. Nathaniel immediately declared that Jesus was the Son of God and the King of Israel. Jesus replied with this fascinating reference back to Jacob: *"Because I said to you, I saw you under the fig tree, do you believe? You will see greater things than these. Most assuredly I say to you, you will see the heavens opened and the angels of God ascending and descending on the Son of Man."*

Here Jesus showed that he was the reality of the ladder that Jacob had dreamed about so many centuries before. From Nathaniel's perspective, it was startling news that Jesus knew him before Nathaniel knew Jesus. Similarly, it is wonderful that Jesus knew us before we knew him. Even knowing who we were, he still died to make us his.

But Jesus was saying, "Yes, that's good news, but listen to this. You're going to see the messengers of God ascending and descending on the Son of Man." Nathaniel was going to see Jesus Christ, the ladder, joining earth and heaven. He would see the glory of God in heaven made available to man on earth. He would see man on earth able to have access to God in heaven. All of that was all going to happen through Christ. Christ is the one who joins heaven and earth.

Where does that happen today? Today, that ladder from heaven (Christ) touches earth in the church, the body of Christ. Remember, Jacob said that the spot where the ladder touched earth was the house of God and the gate of heaven. When God's people on the earth join together under the direct leadership of Christ and allow the rule of heaven to be known on the earth, the reality of Jacob's dream comes into being. Now that's glorious!

Practically speaking, it has always been the Lord's desire that we would learn to fellowship with him in heavenly places. In John 10:9 the Lord said, *"My sheep hear my voice and follow me and they will go in and out and find pasture."* Go in and out of where? Yes, the heavens, the realm of God's presence. We follow the Lord and he leads us into the heavens to fellowship with him and his Father. We go through Jesus Christ to God; we come out to relate to the world. We go in, we go out.

We are to do that because that's what Jesus Christ did. He went into God for sustenance; he came out to interact with the world. He spoke what he heard his Father saying. He did what he knew the Father wanted him to do. How did he know what his Father was doing? How did he hear his Father's words? He was a frequent visitor to heaven. In his Father's heavenly presence, Jesus found real food and real drink. He found sustenance and direction for living in this fallen world. Today, through the Holy Spirit, we can do the same.

Christ Died to Make Us Worthy

Will we be as good at it as Jesus? Not often. We live in fallen bodies and are in the process of having our souls made new. That complete renewal will not be fully accomplished until Christ is fully revealed. Besides that, we are each single members of his body and, on our own, not designed to represent his fullness. As such, we function best when we are in concert with the rest of the body. But we do have his Spirit within us and we will know wonderful moments of sensing our heavenly place in Christ. Paul put it well when he said in Philippians 3, *"Not that I have already become perfect but I press on that I may lay hold of that for which I was laid hold of by Jesus...I press on toward the goal for the prize of the upward call of God in Christ Jesus."* God is calling us upward into his heavenly presence. Let's respond, "Yes, Lord, we're coming!"

Despite that wonderful offer, some people are afraid to approach God. They are afraid they will receive condemnation; they are afraid they will hear their heavenly Father say, "You've really sinned this time." They've bought into the lie that they are not worthy to spend time with their God. They think they don't belong in his heavenly realm. Their thoughts tell them they can't go in there, at least not right now, that God will be mad, disappointed or disgusted with them.

But that is all a lie. Christ died to cleanse us of our sins. Yes, we were guilty; but it is Jesus' righteousness, not our own, which allows us access to God. If you have fallen victim to that mind set, it's time to rise up and claim your true inheritance. You can go in to God's presence and find nourishment for your weary soul. Then you can come out and share that rich food with your fellow believers. That's the church and the gate of heaven. We share the food, the richness and the life that is Christ. When we experience that, Jesus says, then we have seen and tasted something that is truly wonderful.

In II Corinthians 5 the apostle Paul described how this works. Here is what he wrote: *"For we know that if the earthly tent which is our house is torn down, we have a building from God, a house not made with hands, eternal in the heavens."*

Inside of believers there is a building going up. It is a heavenly building, an eternal building. That happens as we fellowship with the Lord, as he builds his life into us. This is our experience in the secret place that Jesus talked about in Matthew 6. God gives us himself when we go to him in the secret place. He works on his eternal building as we fellowship with him. Paul goes on to say in verse 2, *"For indeed in this house we groan longing to be clothed with our dwelling from heaven inasmuch as we having put it on will not be found naked...so that what is mortal will be swallowed by life. Now he who prepared us for this very purpose is God, who gave to us the Spirit as a pledge."*

Have you ever groaned because the weight of the world gets so tiresome? Have you ever longed for Jesus to return and make everything whole? That is because there is a heavenly building going on inside you that is longing for the outside to match the inside.

Because of Christ's presence within you, you have touched heaven, the realm of God's presence. You have tasted the love, peace, joy and fullness that are available to us there.

The amazing thing is that we have been prepared for this very purpose. We have been given the Holy Spirit so that we on earth could access heaven and heaven could access us on earth. When we do that as believers—you and I and all those who make up the house of God—the church becomes the gate to the heavenlies. His body becomes the place on earth through which God touches people. His body becomes the place on earth where his image is displayed and where his enemy's influence is destroyed. That is a dynamic place to be!

Friends, claim your inheritance. Through the blood of Christ, enter the heavenly place where your Father dwells. Invite him to build into you the riches of that realm. Pray with boldness, "Lord, your kingdom come, your will be done, on earth, in me, as it is in the heavens." Be ready for adventure. He will answer that prayer.

The Kingdom of God
"The Father has chosen gladly to give you the kingdom..."

Luke 12:32

What image comes to your mind when you hear the phrase "the kingdom of God"? The image that flashes into my mind is of a poorly dressed, slightly deranged-looking man with a straggly beard. He's standing on a street corner in San Francisco holding a sign reading: "Repent, for the kingdom of God is at hand." That doesn't sound very appealing. In fact, it makes the kingdom of God seem like something to avoid at all costs. God's enemy would love to see that image, or any other negative one of the kingdom of God, abound. He does not want to see the kingdom of God made real. Where it thrives, he is defeated.

Such negative images have nothing to do with the real kingdom of God. God's kingdom is a place of vitality, beauty, riches, glory and humility. We must bring new depth to our understanding of what the word "kingdom" means in order to experience the wonders that are present therein.

The kingdom of God and the heavens are deeply intertwined. The heavens refer to the realm of God's presence, the place where God can be found. As Jesus prayed in Matthew 6:9, *"Our Father, who is in the heavens..."* This is a spiritual realm, invisible to human eyes. God's kingdom refers to all those people and places where his presence is experienced, where his authority is carried out. His kingdom covers realms visible and invisible. There are many

Old Testament references to the heavens. But, significantly, there are no Old Testament references to the kingdom of God. The visible expression of God's kingdom on earth began with Jesus Christ.

From his throne in the heavens, God's purpose is to bring all things under his authority. Hence Jesus' prayer for *"his kingdom to come...on earth as it is in the heavens."* The perfect demonstration of that is the Lord Jesus himself. On earth, he was full of the presence of God. He perfectly carried out God's authority. Here's an example. Jesus cast out a demon from a blind man, fully healing him. Then he said, *"If I cast out demons by the Spirit of God, then the kingdom of God has come upon you"* (Matthew 12:28).

When Christ came, the kingdom of God came with him. Through him we can now enter into and participate in the building of this kingdom. As we learn to dwell in Christ, we experience the rule of God. Our lives express his kingdom rule. In the process, that which is Godly, spiritual and eternal in nature becomes visible in the physical world.

Kingdoms of This Earth

Kings must have a domain over which they rule. That is their kingdom. God's instructions to Adam show that a specific part of Adam's responsibility was to rule over this planet. *"And God said, Let us make man in our image, after our likeness, and let them rule over the fish of the sea and over the birds of the air and over the cattle and over all the earth and over every creeping thing that creeps on the earth"* (Genesis 1: 26). Exercising authority is part of what it means to be made in God's image. From the beginning, God designed man to have dominion over this planet. He purposed that man would rule in his image. God desired that earth would experience the benefit of that rule. This meant that God's authority would be manifest throughout creation.

Where would man get the power to exercise that authority? Authority is a function of the strength of life. As cats dominate mice and dogs dominate cats, higher life forms dominate lower life forms.

To reflect God's authority and express his image on the earth, man needed the power of the life of God. In order for man to rule properly, God made his life available to Adam in the garden. He put that life in the tree of life.

But Adam chose to eat from the wrong tree. He failed to take in the life that had the authority to defeat God's enemy. Rather, Adam and Eve ate of the forbidden tree of the knowledge of good and evil. They surrendered their right to rule to the enemy who had deceived them. In so doing, their unity with God was broken. Self-awareness and shame replaced open fellowship with God and self-less unity with one another. That unity has been broken ever since.

There have been many down through the ages who could claim that they have ruled portions of this planet. But that rule has not often been influenced by the authority of a loving God. That rule has not brought the benefits of God's heavenly realm to a world lost in darkness. But behind the scenes God is building a more glorious kingdom than any to be seen on the earth. His rule is more benevolent than any offered by a temporal king or government.

Bringing in the rule of God takes the life of God. The rule of God results in unity among those who receive that life. We will see in this chapter how God accomplishes that in Christ. We will see what our part is in the fulfillment of his purpose. God has chosen to share his kingdom rule with you and me. He is not going to fulfill his purpose without us.

It All Starts with Christ

The opening verse of Matthew's gospel reads, *"The book of the genealogy of Jesus Christ, the son of David, the son of Abraham."* First impressions are important. Jesus Christ was introduced as the son of David because David was known as the greatest king of Israel. Throughout Israel's history the king's throne in Israel was called the throne of David. He was a man after God's own heart. The first thing we find out about Jesus Christ is that he is royalty. Your Lord is a King. Not just a King…the King of Kings.

Secondly, Jesus was described as the son of Abraham. Abraham fathered the nation of Israel. Abraham has a double meaning: he is "the one who crossed over" and the "father of nations." Abraham was the first one to leave the old world behind. He crossed over the Jordan as the father of a new nation in a new land. With Abraham you have the promise of a new land with a new nation in it. In Jesus Christ, God brought in the king of a new kingdom. But he was not coming alone. He is the beginning of a whole new nation. That's exciting news.

In Matthew 2:2 the three wise men looking for the baby Jesus asked, *"Where is he that is born King of the Jews? For we have seen his star in the east, and have come to worship him."* From his very birth, Jesus was called the King of the Jews. When Jesus entered Jerusalem shortly before his crucifixion, the crowds shouted out, *"Hosanna: Blessed is the King of Israel that comes in the name of the Lord."* When the Lord stood before Pilate, Pilate said, *"Are you a king then? Jesus answered; you say that I am a king. To this end was I born, and for this cause came I into the world, that I should bear witness unto the truth."* The truth is that Jesus is the King of Kings. Even in his crucifixion, the truth was told. Though hung in a mocking way, Luke tells us that, *"a sign above him read in letters of Greek, and Latin, and Hebrew, This is the King of the Jews..."*

Most believers know full well that Jesus came to be a King. But we should not overlook the practical significance of that. Watch how this theme is developed in Matthew's gospel. Matthew 3:1-3 says, *"In those days, John the baptizer came preaching in the wilderness of Judea saying, 'Repent, for the kingdom of heaven is at hand' for this is the one referred to by Isaiah the prophet saying, the voice of one crying in the wilderness make ready the way of the Lord, make his paths straight."*

John quoted a verse in Isaiah 40:3 that said, *"make smooth a highway for our God."* God needed a highway because he had somewhere he wanted to go. He wanted to do some traveling. He wanted to get to earth. When he arrived there, he wanted to rule! He was going to do that through Jesus Christ. John was letting people know they should get ready. With the coming of Christ there was an invasion of this earth by the kingdom of God.

John was the first to announce the coming kingdom. He prepared hearts to receive the coming King. Watch what happens when Jesus begins his public ministry. Matthew 4:17 says, *"From that time Jesus began to preach, and to say, Repent: for the kingdom of heaven is at hand."* When Jesus began to preach he also announced that the kingdom was coming. Notice that both John and Jesus emphasized the need for repentance in receiving this kingdom.

The Role of Repentance

Repentance is key to entering the kingdom of God. Repentance opens the door for the coming Lord. It is our first step in seeing the kingdom made real in our lives. We turn away from our old lifestyle of sin and separation from God. Some Christians, however, live in a mode of continual repentance. They are so aware of their sinfulness that they feel bogged down and defeated. They spend their whole lives repenting over their sins to the point where they become fixated on their condition rather than on the King and his kingdom. If you are one who has been stuck there, take heart. It's time to move on.

John the baptizer told people to repent for the kingdom was near. Then the kingdom arrived in person! Repentance was necessary because everything that came before was finished. Man had failed in his ability to please God. That was no secret. Now God was done relating to his people through rules, through the Old Testament laws, and through the old priesthood with its robes, rituals and sacrifices. It was time to turn away from all of that. This is what repentance is: a turning away from the old and an embracing of the new.

In Jesus Christ, God moved from the pictures of the Old Testament to reality. The nation of Israel had been raised up by God as a foreshadowing of what was to come. Though Adam and Eve had failed in their responsibility, God wanted a people on the earth to whom he could express his goodness and through whom he could have an expression of his nature on the planet. God desired to personally lead that people, the nation of Israel, through his presence in the Tabernacle, but the people demanded a king. Samuel reported in 1 Samuel 10:19, *"But you have today rejected your God, who delivers you from all your calamities and your distresses; yet you have said, No, but set a king over us."* So God answered their request and gave them earthly kings, starting with Saul.

But God's kingdom is not like worldly kingdoms. His kingdom is based on a new way of relating to him. Other than using the Old Testament experience as a picture of what was to come, our New Testament experience has nothing to do with how the Jews practiced their religion. His kingdom is made up of Jew and Gentile, not just one race or nation. This is why John could announce the news that the old way was over with. The people needed to repent because something new was coming. That something new was the Lord Jesus himself. When he arrived, John said, *"We beheld his glory, glory as of the only begotten from the Father full of grace and truth."* A new day had dawned.

Jesus Christ showed up, revealing the true nature of God's kingdom and exercising the authority of the living God. This was not a kingdom based on rules, but one based on relationship with God himself. Yes, you have to repent to receive him, but repentance is the door, not the dwelling place. Let's go through repentance and into the kingdom. Let's have the experience of that kingdom change the way we relate to God and the way we relate to others. Repentance alone will not and cannot permanently change our lives, but experience with Christ in his kingdom can.

The Kingdom Is Dangerous

Matthew 4:23 says, *"Jesus went about all Galilee, teaching in their synagogues, and preaching the gospel of the kingdom, and healing all manner of sickness and all manner of disease among the people."* The Lord took his life into his hands when he declared the new kingdom. The people of Israel already had a King when Jesus arrived. They were enslaved by the Roman Empire and its Caesar. Under the Romans, Herod was ruling as the King over the Jewish people. It is difficult for Americans to relate to the danger inherent in what Jesus was doing. It would be like someone going to Saudi Arabia and announcing there was a new king coming, and he was that king. The palace guards would immediately imprison and likely kill him, because they already have a king. Earthly kings do not suffer opposition well. The news from the wise men that a king had been born in Bethlehem was enough to drive King Herod to have thousands of babies slain throughout Israel in his attempt to eliminate competition for his throne.

The Lord said in Matthew 11:12, *"And from the days of John until now the kingdom of heaven suffers violence, and the violent take it by force."* When it comes to the kingdom, there will be battles involved. Jesus made it clear, however, that the real conflict would be fought in the heavens. As he said in John 18:36, *"My kingdom is not of this world: if my kingdom were of this world, then my servants would be fighting, that I might not be delivered to the Jews: but now is my kingdom not of this realm."* The kingdom of God does not advance using earthly weapons, such as swords and cannon. It is not based in an earthly quest for land and power.

Paul backed this up in chapter 6 of Ephesians: *"Finally, my brethren, be strong in the Lord, and in the strength of his might. Put on the full armor of God, that you may be able to stand firm against the schemes of the devil for we wrestle not against flesh and blood, but against the rulers, against the powers, against the world forces of this darkness, against the spiritual forces of wickedness in heavenly places."* That's kingdom talk.

When I was a young believer living in Isla Vista, California, our church fellowship made a large banner that read, "Jesus Christ is Lord of Isla Vista." We hung it between two flag poles that were about twenty-five feet in the air. We simply wanted to make a statement to our community about the One we believed in. It was perhaps an "in your face" approach to evangelism. But certainly not as bold as some of the things Jesus did.

Everyone in that community could see it as they went back and forth to the university in that town. The reaction in the city was very interesting. One of our neighbors hung out a sign that read, "Lions eat Christians." Then the local officials passed a law against large signs hanging on flag poles. After a while, when we wouldn't take it down, we were threatened with arrest and jail time. Eventually, our point made, we gave in and took it down. Interestingly enough, shortly thereafter a local newspaper took a poll to see who really was Lord of Isla Vista. Though none of us participated, Jesus Christ still won. The point is that the enemy never wants his rule openly threatened by the exaltation of Jesus Christ. Not in the first century, not today.

Nevertheless, Jesus continually advanced the cause of his kingdom. In Luke 4:43, Jesus said, *"I must preach the kingdom of God to other cities also: for I was sent for this purpose."* In Matthew 6:31-33 he said this: *"Do not be anxious then, saying, what shall we eat or what shall we drink or with what shall we clothe ourselves? For all these things the Gentiles eagerly seek, for your heavenly Father knows that you need all these things. But seek first his kingdom and his righteousness and all these things shall be added to you."*

For Jesus Christ, this kingdom was very important. If he was sent for the purpose of preaching about it, how central must the kingdom be in the mind of God! That being the case, how do we seek it? We start by knowing where it is. At that moment in time, the extent of the kingdom of God on the earth began and ended with Jesus Christ. Wherever he was, that was the extent of God's presence on the earth. To seek the kingdom was to seek after Jesus Christ.

We See the Kingdom in Christ

Jesus Christ personally brought the activity of God to earth. If you were with him, you were with God. E. Stanley Jones wrote, "It's very hard to know God, or imagine what he's like, but Christ is the image of God. My God has got to resemble Jesus Christ. Not the other way around. If my God is not like Christ, I don't want him." Many people are afraid of God. But they are not afraid of Christ. They need to see their God in the light of Christ, for he is the image of God.

A highly esteemed Christian leader from Nepal, who had suffered much for his faith, put it this way: "If Jesus is not in heaven, I don't want to be there either." Thank God, he is there and we can be there with him. He is glorious and full of love because he allowed the gracious rule of God and God's glorious presence to dominate his entire being.

Jesus Christ healed the sick, cured diseases and taught the multitudes knowing that he was the extent of the kingdom of God on the planet. He did not expect to find it anywhere else. He told people to seek God's kingdom and his righteousness. Today the righteousness of God is found in Christ. He is the one who gives us standing before God. We live in the kingdom of God by seeking Christ, by living in his presence, by taking him as our righteousness. When we are anxious about all the cares that the world continually throws at us, we should seek the Lord Jesus. He has the power and the authority to deliver us from the cares of this world.

Matthew 9:35 says, *"And Jesus went about all the cities and villages, teaching in their synagogues, and preaching the gospel of the kingdom, and healing every sickness and every disease among the people."* Here again we see Jesus emphasizing that the kingdom had come. Then Jesus sent out the twelve and instructed them, *"And as you go, preach, saying, the kingdom of heaven is at hand"* (Matthew 10:7). Their message was to be the same as his.

We discussed in the chapter on heaven the Lord's amazing words in Matthew 16 regarding the keys to the kingdom of heaven. We need the Lord to reveal to us the reality that his kingdom is in our midst. The gospel of the kingdom overrides so many of our petty concerns. The kingdom is not defined by where you go to church, or what your perspective is on the Holy Spirit, or whether or not you believe in tongues, or whether you baptize by sprinkling or immersion or at all. When we are talking about the kingdom, we transcend that which divides us. When we can catch the vision that we are first and foremost citizens of God's kingdom and put ourselves under his rule, new doors are opened to the expansion of that kingdom and all its glorious riches.

Seeing that God's purpose is to bring the reality of his kingdom to this earth through his people changes how believers relate to one another. Believers may have different backgrounds, but they all have something in common. They share the same purpose. Such revelation encourages believers to strive to keep the unity of the body. Without that unity God's rule cannot be effectively carried out. If we can see this kingdom and understand its relevance and see its fruit, we can truly be a part of opening a highway for our God, allowing him to make a home and establish his kingdom in our midst.

The Kingdom Expands

During his final meal before his crucifixion the Lord said this to his friends in Luke 22: *"I have earnestly desired to eat this Passover with you before I suffer for I say to you I shall not eat it again until it is fulfilled in the kingdom of God, And when he had taken a cup and given thanks, he said, Take this and share it among yourselves for I say to you I will not drink of the fruit of the vine from now on until the kingdom of God comes."* The Lord was aware that up to the time of his death, he alone manifested the kingdom of God. He alone lived under the rule of his Father and bore the image of God on the earth. But all that was about to change. The Lord knew that no one could enter the realm of his Father's presence without the righteousness of God. Through his death, the real Passover would cleanse us by the shed blood of God's Lamb. That would allow cleansed sinners to come to God and receive his life. The way to the tree of life would be open again. This would be accomplished by the sacrifice of the Son because the Son was willing to surrender himself to the will of the Father so that we could enter his kingdom.

That is why Jesus Christ so earnestly looked forward to eating this Passover meal with his followers. The Passover is the most well documented Old Testament ceremony. For a Jew it represented passing from death to life and marked the celebration of the birth of the nation of Israel. In the Passover God's people were delivered out of Egypt and out of death. Jesus Christ knew this.

He had come out of the kingdom of heaven to bring the rule of that kingdom to earth. He knew that he was the seed of a new nation. He knew that his death, the real Passover sacrifice, would set mankind free from sin and open the realm of heaven to them. So he sat with his disciples and said, "I have really been looking forward to this occasion with you, because the next time we do this it will be for real." The Lord knew that his body and blood were the reality of the bread and wine that would make that kingdom available to them.

They handled this glorious, deep news with typical decorum. They immediately got into a fight over who was going to be the greatest in the coming kingdom. The fact that they didn't yet have a clue about what he was talking about should give us some comfort. These deep truths of God often take time to be understood.

But Jesus Christ knew the full meaning of all that had gone before and all that was coming. He knew that the millions of Passover lambs that had been slaughtered over the years were a picture of his death. He knew that the sheaf of wheat that was waved before God in the festival of Firstfruits was a symbol of his resurrection. He knew that all the loaves that had been baked out of crushed wheat and placed before the altar of God in the ceremony of Pentecost were a symbol of the new human that would be created out of both Jew and Gentile. He was fully aware that through his death the glorious and gracious rule of his Father would be extended to the man God had created. He knew that through that rule the subsequent defeat of the powers of darkness was inevitable. Yes, Jesus eagerly looked forward to this Passover. Though it signaled his imminent and excruciating death, Jesus was able to give thanks to his Father that it was at hand. The fulfilling of the Passover meant the full realization of the kingdom!

Jesus had gone all over Israel preaching the kingdom of God. He knew that a kingdom had come out of heaven, out of God, to be made visible on this earth. He knew that the kingdom was about to be birthed among his followers and that it was going to take his death and resurrection to make it possible.

Looking back, we can surely say that the crucifixion, the resurrection, the glorification and the dispensing of Jesus Christ into his followers accomplished atonement. His blood, the wine poured out, is sufficient for our sins.

We can also declare that the breaking of his body, the real bread, brought life to his people and made entrance into the kingdom of God available to them. The breaking of his body and the shedding of his blood delivered people out of sin and into Christ.

Jesus looked forward to eating this Passover with his followers and friends because it was the last time he would eat it as a picture. This was the last time the bread and wine would be only symbolic. Pictures were on their way out, because the next time he ate it with his friends, it would be fulfilled in the kingdom of God. That's why Paul could write many years later to the believers in Corinth, *"If any man is in Christ, he is a new creation; old things have passed away, new things have come!"* (II Corinthians 5:17). Those new things are the things available to us in the kingdom of God!

Imagine the Lord's joy following his death and resurrection when he returned to the upper room and walked through a locked door to once again meet, fellowship, eat and drink with his followers and friends, soon to be his brothers and sisters. The first thing he did when he came back into that room was to breathe his life into his disciples. In those amazing moments we see the initial expansion of the Kingdom of God. Jesus Christ, by breathing his Spirit into his disciples, was literally putting the access road to the realm of the heavens, the highway that John spoke of, into the hearts of his followers!

They surely didn't understand all that was happening to them at that moment. Jesus Christ understood it, though. Later on, when the resurrected Christ sat down with his followers to break bread and drink wine, they no doubt rejoiced that the kingdom had come in them. Peter referred to this in Acts 10:40 when he wrote, *"God raised him up on the third day and granted that he become visible not to all the people but to witnesses who were chosen beforehand by God,* **to us who ate and drank with him after he arose from the dead.***"* The Lord had come to live in his people, and his mission of establishing the kingdom had been fulfilled. The Lord and his friends ate and rejoiced.

But their fellowship didn't end there. Kingdom talk was just getting underway. We see this in Acts 1:3: *"To these Jesus also presented himself alive, after his suffering, by many convincing proofs, appearing to them over a period of forty days and speaking of the things concerning the kingdom of*

God." Obviously they weren't talking about something that was going to come into existence thousands of years later at the end of time. They were talking about its practicality then, in their midst. God's kingdom had come to earth and it was not leaving. The Lord remained with them for forty days, talking to them about what it was going to be like following him in spirit rather than in flesh. He may have talked to them about how to deal with the enemy in prayer, what it would mean to deny their fallen natures, and how to turn away from old habits and live by him. Perhaps he showed them how to use the words of the Psalms to go into the presence of God, how to experience deep worship and how to share life with each other on a daily basis. He spent that time sharing with them what it would be like as they learned to live in his Kingdom by his Spirit.

Listen to the Lord's words in Matthew 28:18, at the end of those forty days: *"All authority has been given to me in heaven and on earth, go then and make disciples, baptizing them into the Name of the Father and the Son and the Holy Spirit, teaching them to keep all that I am directing you, and lo, I am with you always, even to the end of the age."* The Lord Jesus had been given all authority in heaven and on earth. That's kingdom talk. If you go to heaven, he is in authority there; if you are on the earth, he is in authority there. Praise God, the Lord Jesus passed this authority on to his followers.

That authority was in them individually through his breathing his Spirit into them in the upper room. It would soon be on them corporately through the anointing of the Holy Spirit on the day of Pentecost. As they went out into the world sharing the reality of what had happened to them, his kingdom and rule would soon be spreading throughout Palestine and even to the ends of the earth. His rule would extend to people everywhere who repented and received Jesus Christ. What Jesus could not accomplish in human form, he could now do throughout the inhabited earth by means of his Spirit. What a wise plan!

New Generations Enter the Kingdom

When we think of kingdoms we think of authority and of rule. We think of battles won and lost, of victories shared and ground gained. Jesus Christ came to bring the rule of heaven and the reality of God's presence to earth. As Hebrews 2:10 says, *"For it was fitting for him (God), for whom are all things, and through whom are all things, in bringing many sons to glory, to make the captain of their salvation (Jesus) perfect through sufferings."* As our captain, Jesus Christ announced the coming of the kingdom of God. His plan was to bring many sons into the glory of this kingdom. When he sent his disciples out, they spread the good news of this kingdom. As they met following his resurrection, once again they spoke of the kingdom.

Jesus continued to teach his followers about the kingdom because now they were in it. In fact, they would be the vehicle by which he would continue to expand the kingdom of God in the hearts of people everywhere. Acts 8:12 described this scene in Samaria: *"But when they believed Philip preaching the things concerning the kingdom of God, and the name of Jesus Christ, they were baptized, both men and women."* The kingdom was growing!

Paul got into the act in Acts 14:22, where he was *"confirming the souls of the disciples, and exhorting them to continue in the faith, and that we must through much tribulation enter into the kingdom of God."* In Acts 19:8, when Paul got to Ephesus, *"he went into the synagogue, and spoke boldly for three months, reasoning and persuading them about the kingdom of God."*

If Paul spent three months talking about the kingdom of God, there must be a lot to learn about it. But if that seems like a lot of emphasis on the kingdom, check out what happened in Rome. There, Paul *"stayed two full years in his own rented quarters and was welcoming all who came to him, preaching the kingdom of God and teaching concerning the Lord Jesus Christ with all openness, unhindered"* (Acts 28:30). This is a dynamic combination, the kingdom of God and the Lord Jesus Christ. From God's perspective, the two are eternally intertwined.

Widening our Boundaries

The kingdom of God is much bigger than what our minds can conceive. In that respect, believers too often limit their connection to the kingdom of God to their particular church affiliation. Theologically like-minded church members are the only ones they fellowship with, work with and support. For some, the kingdom of God and their church are synonymous. All others are outside the camp.

While intimate connection to a distinct group of believers is necessary for healthy Christian living, we ought not to confine our thinking about God's kingdom to denominational boxes. Doing so has led to great division in the body of Christ. It's time to lift our eyes and see the overarching kingdom of God, that kingdom that has its roots in eternity past and stretches out into eternity future. It is entrance into that kingdom that is ultimately important. It is advancing the agenda of that kingdom that should take precedence in our relationships with others. If we are in the kingdom, that is what matters. In God's kingdom an eternal, divine connectedness exists among all believers in Christ regardless of our denominational affiliation or style of church practice.

Preaching the gospel of the kingdom is still Jesus' mission today, one that he is carrying out in you and in me. He is our King. He is our ruler. He is the one who brings the kingdom to bear in our lives. As we submit to him both individually and as communities of faith, the will of God can be expressed on this earth. Now we can pray with him, "Father, your kingdom's come, your will's begun, on earth as it is in heaven."

One day all creation will see Christ's glorious mission completed. As Paul wrote in 1 Corinthians 15:24, *"Then comes the end, when he (Jesus) delivers up the kingdom to God, even the Father; when he has abolished all rule and all authority and power for he must reign until he has put all enemies under his feet. The last enemy to be abolished is death."*

The apostle John reported the onset of that great day in Revelation 12:10, when he wrote, *"And I heard a loud voice saying in heaven, Now is come salvation, and strength, and the kingdom of our God, and the power of his Christ: for the accuser of our brethren is cast down, who accuses them before our God day and night."*

We have a part in this divine drama. Jesus Christ brought the rule of heaven into our hearts through his Holy Spirit. By his Spirit he is now building a kingdom that cannot be shaken by the enemy's accusations and threats; no, not even by death itself. He is building a kingdom that bears the image of God and carries out the rule of God. This is the corporate man that God had in mind way back in Genesis 1. Will you turn your heart to the Lord today and invite him to reign in your life? Will you ask him to connect you with others who are doing the same? These are the building blocks of kingdom living. May they be so in our experience.

The Spirit

"Unless you are born of water and the Spirit ..." John 3:5

In our last chapter we examined God's purpose in establishing his heavenly kingdom here on earth. Thankfully, God has designed a practical way to build that kingdom that allows us to partake and participate in it. Central to our understanding and experience of that kingdom is the role of the Holy Spirit.

Many believers are unclear about the person and role of the Spirit. If you are one of them, this chapter was written to help you sort through the confusion and open to you a richer relationship with your Lord. Doctrinal differences over the meaning of the Baptism of the Holy Spirit and the modern-day practice of the gifts of the Spirit, for example, have divided and perplexed believers. As a result, many followers of Christ have been scared away from an active relationship with the Spirit. Not surprisingly, they are often left with a Christian experience that lacks vitality. Other believers embrace the things of the Spirit with fervent emotion, looking to have some kind of special manifestation that proves their devotion to Christ. The danger is that believers can become emotionally dependent on such manifestations, substituting them for a deeper experience with Christ. Over time, emotions run dry, leaving believers who were fueled by them looking for more from their Christian walk.

The recovery of a Biblical understanding of the Spirit is crucial to a revitalized experience of Christ, both for us personally and in our corporate fellowships. While a whole book could have been devoted to this single topic, as many have been, my goal in this chapter is simply to open the Scriptures to reveal a way of thinking about and relating to the Spirit that will take the reader deeper into Christ.

The Importance of the Spirit

Consider these words spoken by the Lord Jesus to Nicodemus in John 3: 5: *"Jesus answered, truly, truly, I say to you, unless one is born of water and of the Spirit, he cannot enter into the kingdom of God. That which is born of the flesh is flesh; and that which is born of the Spirit is Spirit."* If we are going to enter the kingdom of God, we must be born of the Spirit. That means that access to the kingdom is only possible through the Spirit. John the Baptizer said, *"I am baptizing in repentance, but the one that comes afterwards, he will baptize in the Holy Spirit."* Repentance clears the way for us to begin a new relationship with our God. It's time to turn away from our human efforts to reach God. It's time to turn away from dead ritual and formulaic religion. A new relationship, born in repentance, is carried out in the Spirit.

Jesus' mission as introduced by John was integrally related to his followers being baptized or, perhaps more aptly translated, immersed, in this Spirit. John didn't say that Jesus was going to immerse some in the Spirit and not others. Nor do the Scriptures say that being immersed in the Spirit is a second blessing of some kind, reserved for those who are really serious about following Christ. As Paul wrote to the Corinthians, *"For **by one Spirit are we all baptized** into one body, whether we be Jews or Gentiles, whether we be bond or free; and **have been all made to drink into one Spirit**"* (I Corinthians 12:13).

Baptizing or immersing all of his followers in the Holy Spirit is central to Jesus' purpose in coming to this planet. That, as we shall see, is glorious news. It highlights the importance of understanding the work of the Spirit in our lives.

So who is this Spirit, and how does he work?

A good place to start might be to ask what your comfort level is with respect to the Holy Spirit. That may seem uncomfortable to some, but there's purpose to it. If you had to rate your level of comfort regarding God the Father, God the Son and God the Holy Spirit, which one would you say that you are more drawn to? Is there one in the Godhead that you feel more comfortable with, one that you would consider as having a higher level of importance in your life as a Christian?

When this question is asked in Christian settings, inevitably, those present answer that they feel most comfortable with the Son, the Lord Jesus. Most people feel drawn to the Son. This is totally understandable. The Lord Jesus is the one who put on human flesh and whose life we see recorded in the gospels. The Lord Jesus is the One who died for our sins. The Lord Jesus is the One who has given us new life.

What often happens, however, is that people tend to identify only with the Jesus of the Gospels. He's the Jesus that walked on earth, the Jesus that changed water into wine, and the Jesus on the cross. They tend to associate Jesus primarily with the physical human being that walked the dusty roads of Galilee in the first century.

But is that all there is to what God wants you to understand about Jesus? Or is there a more intimate way to relate to him that believers have underutilized because they have not seen the totality of his great work? They love Jesus, they understand Jesus, but they don't understand the Spirit very well, so they just don't go there. If you can relate to that, I hope this chapter will help you increase your comfort level with this divine Spirit.

God is Comfortable as Spirit

Let's first understand that God the Father has always been Spirit. He is absolutely comfortable being Spirit, and he expects that we will become comfortable in knowing him as he is. Jesus emphasized this in John 4:24 when he said, *"God is Spirit and those who worship him must worship him in Spirit and in truth."* Before God the

Son became incarnate, he was also Spirit. These two were gloriously one.

The apostle John wrote in the first chapter of his gospel, *"In the beginning was the Word and the Word was toward God and the Word was God. He was in the beginning with God. All things came into being through him and apart from him nothing came into being that has come into being...and the Word became flesh and dwelt among us."* It was through this divine Word that God created the universe and, wondrously enough, one day this Word became flesh as the incarnate Son of God, Jesus Christ.

Prior to his incarnation, this divine Word was Spirit. And out of his spiritual richness, the vast variety of the universe came into being. When we see the incredible beauty of the creation, we should be mindful that its inspiration came out of invisible realms. As the writer of Hebrews put it, *"By faith we understand that the worlds were prepared by the Word of God so that what is seen was not made out of things which are visible"* (Heb. 11:3).

The realm of the Spirit and the realm of the physical have always been intertwined in the plan of God. In Genesis 1, the Spirit of God was present, moving over the face of the waters. And out of this glorious Spirit came the created universe. Its complexity only hints at the variety and richness in our God. Do you love sunsets? Those sunsets portray something of the spiritual richness of God. Do you love horses or dogs or waterfalls or moonlit nights? All the qualities that make them lovable or beautiful or enchanting were born out of his vibrant being. The wonder of it all is that God desires to offer the riches of his Spirit-filled realm to us.

But therein lies a problem. God is Spirit. But what is man? According to Genesis 2:7, *"The Lord God formed man of dust from the ground and breathed into his nostrils the breath of life and man became a living soul."*

God in his essence is Divine Spirit. Man in his created essence is soul. The apostle Paul refers to this when he says in I Corinthians 15:45, *"The first man Adam was made a living soul."* Soul can be defined as the human personality made up of those characteristics of mind, emotion, and will that motivate human beings. Adam's human soul was encased in a body made of earth that we call flesh. In fact, the word "Adam" meant red clay.

How will a God who is Spirit transmit the riches of his realm to a man who is soul? Or, to put it another way, who will bridge the gap between Spirit and soul? In the Genesis creation the answer lay in God's provision of the tree of life. God placed his very own life into the Garden in the wondrous tree of life. He invited man to eat of every tree of the garden except the tree of the knowledge of good and evil. If man had partaken of the tree of life and taken into himself the life contained therein, he would have had access to the very riches of God himself. But man failed to do this and ate instead of the forbidden tree of the knowledge of good and evil. Man fell from his high position as God's selected image-bearer and God closed the way to the tree of life. In the process man lost his connection to God and became preoccupied with the physical and earthly.

Thus began the history of mankind. But God never wavered in his purpose of making the riches of his spirit realm available to his creation. The fullness of that plan was realized in time with the coming of Jesus Christ. As we have discussed in previous chapters, Jesus brought the reality of God's realm to earth. His birth, life, death and resurrection were the glorious product of a human life saturated by the divine life of the Spirit of God. He was God come in flesh, the image of the invisible God. But how would God's purpose play out following the ascension of Christ?

Jesus Shows the Way

Understanding the difficulty with which earthly-minded humans grasp spiritual realities, just before Jesus went to the cross he sought to help his disciples prepare for what was ahead. He said, *"I will ask the Father and he will give you another Helper that he may be with you forever, the Spirit of Truth, whom the world cannot receive, because it does not see him or know him;* **you know him because he abides with you and will be in you. I will not leave you as orphans, I will come to you***"* (John 14:16-18).

71

Jesus made it plain to his disciples that though he would be physically leaving them, help was on the way. He had not simply given them a model by which to live, so that now that they had seen Jesus in action, they should be able to do the same things. No. The Spirit of Truth was coming, who would never leave them. But who was this Spirit of Truth that Jesus would give this important task to? Look at his words: *"You know him because he abides with you and will be in you...I will come to you."* Yes, the Spirit of Truth is Jesus, himself.

While that is a statement we may have often heard, the issue is the degree to which we allow this truth to impact our lives. To what degree do we let it impact our relationship with the Spirit? The answer to that question can change your life and the lives of those around you!

Listen to Jesus' words in John 17:22-24: *"The glory which you have given Me, I have given to them, that they may be one, just as We are one, I in them and You in Me, that they may be perfected in unity so that the world may know that you sent me and loved them even as you have loved me. Father I desire that they also whom you have given me be with me where I am so that they may see my glory which you have given me for you loved me before the foundation of the world."*

These incredibly mysterious and deep words make it clear who is going to be in us. Jesus says, *"I in them."* It was always Jesus' intention to make the realm of the spiritual accessible to those who would believe in him so that they could continue to see him. Jesus is not in us simply to occupy space. He is not in us simply to forgive us of our sins. No. he wants to take us where he is, into his Father's heavenly presence. Now.

Listen to this description of Jesus in John 7:37: *"Now on the last day, the great day of the feast, Jesus stood and cried out saying, If anyone is thirsty, let him come to me and drink. He who believes in me, as the Scripture says, from his innermost being will flow rivers of living water. But this he spoke of the Spirit, whom those who believed in him were to receive; the Spirit was not yet given, because Jesus was not yet glorified."*

An important connection is drawn here between the Spirit being given and Jesus being glorified.

Consider the context. The weeklong Feast of Booths was coming to an end. The Jews had been eating and drinking for days. Jesus knew that satisfaction could not be found simply in outward, earthly pleasures. He knew there was deep thirst in the human soul for something that went beyond the physical, the earthly. In the same way, he knows that in your soul there is a longing for things spiritual, for things divine. That longing has been present in the human soul since the day of its creation so long ago.

Jesus stood and invited all who were thirsty for real life to come to him. He is the source of our water of life. He is our drink, our sustenance. But he was not talking about himself in physical form. He was not inviting people to come to the earthly Jesus, the Jesus who walked in Galilee. No, he was inviting those who thirst for real water to come to the Spirit. He was talking about water that would be drunk in Spirit. He, himself, would be that water! But this Spirit was not yet available to them, for Jesus was not yet glorified. We'll return to these mysterious words later.

Who Will Lead God's People?

Consider the Lord's words in John 10 starting in verse 2: *"he who enters by the door is a shepherd of the sheep. To him the doorkeeper opens and the sheep hear his voice and he calls his own sheep by name and leads them out. When he puts forth all his own he goes ahead of them and the sheep follow him because they know his voice...v.10:I am the good shepherd, the good shepherd lays down his life for the sheep...v.16 I have other sheep who are not of this flock, I must bring them also and they shall hear my voice and they shall become one flock with one shepherd. For this reason the Father loves me, because I lay down my life that I may take it again."*

Jesus is the good shepherd. Those who follow him will hear his voice. That is how he will lead them. He knows all their names. This is very personal and very precious. Jesus laid down his life to achieve the awesome ability to lead each of his followers in this most direct of ways. This didn't pertain to only the Jewish believers who followed him around Galilee. The Lord had other sheep that were not Jewish that he wanted to hear his voice; that he longed to lead into heavenly, spiritual realms. You are one of those sheep. Has he called your name? Have you heard his voice? He laid down his life and took it back again so that you might.

But there is a mystery here. How will the earthly Jesus become the spiritual water of life? How will the earthly Jesus speak to those born in later ages, leading them into his gracious presence?

Here's the answer.

Christ, the Life Giving Spirit

Paul described it in I Corinthians 15:45: *"The first man Adam became a living soul; the last Adam, a life giving Spirit."* God the Father desired to fill the universe with the riches that are contained in his wondrous being. Those riches were stored in his Son, Jesus Christ, come in the flesh, born as the Son of Man. In Christ, the living God could enter the realm of the physical and create a means of access to the divine.

But God had two problems. First, man was created a living soul and needed a way to access spiritual realms. Second, when man fell he became sinful. In such a state he could never gain entrance into the presence of a holy God. When a sinless Christ was crucified for us, he took away our sins. Those accepting his shed blood have a remedy for the second problem.

To deal with the first problem, in Christ's resurrection and ascension, his earthly body was transformed to the point where the physical no longer constrained him. He could walk through a closed and locked door as if it were not there. The early disciples saw this happening before their very eyes. We see the story laid out for us in what they wrote. Watch Jesus' interactions with his followers following his resurrection. Here's the story. Mary came to the tomb to weep over the Lord she had lost. The One she had come to love with all her heart had been taken from her forever. Or so she thought. She saw the stone rolled away and feared that the body had been taken. She was intensely distraught. She couldn't hold back her tears. She saw someone whom she mistook for the gardener. When she asked him where they had taken her Lord, the resurrected Christ turned and called her name: *"Mary."*

Mary instantly recognized the tenderness and familiarity in her Lord's voice. She ran to him and clung to him, holding on with all her might, just as you would do if you had lost the person you loved most in the world and suddenly, miraculously, that person had returned to you. But listen to Jesus' surprising words: *"Stop clinging to me, for I have not yet ascended to my Father, but go to my brethren and say to them, I ascend to my Father and your Father and my God and your God."* (John 20:17) Through Jesus' death and resurrection, the family of God had expanded. What amazing news!

Mary did as she was told. She ran to let the other disciples know of this wonderful news. The Lord was alive! Meanwhile the Lord Jesus did just what he said he was going to do. The resurrected Christ ascended to his Father. There in the Father's presence, in front of the angelic host, Jesus Christ, who called himself the Son of Man while he walked on the earth, was welcomed as the glorified Son of God. He who had walked in human flesh was fully transformed into the glory that he had known with the Father before the earth was formed. His human body was made spiritually divine and, before powers and principalities, the Son of Man was declared to be the Son of God.

As Paul described it to the Romans, *"Paul a bond-servant of Christ Jesus, called as an apostle, set apart for the gospel of God, which he promised beforehand through his prophets in the holy Scriptures, concerning his Son who was born of the seed of David according to the flesh who was declared the Son of God with power by the resurrection from the dead according to the Spirit of holiness, Jesus Christ our Lord"* (Rom. 1:1-4).

Praise God, a divine human, our king Jesus, is now on the throne. This is tremendously significant for us. We, who are human, now have the possibility—no, more than that, the expectation—that through our faith in Christ, we, too, will be glorified in him. What a great work God wrought in Jesus Christ! As a popular hymn put it,

"Our God is a Man, Hallelujah,

A Man who's Divine, Praise his Name,

No longer I roam; my heart's found its home,

I walk and I talk with the King."

Paul put it this way to the Ephesians: *"...in accordance with the working of the strength of his* [God's] *might which he brought about in Christ when he raised him from the dead and seated him at his right hand in the heavenlies, far above all rule and authority and power and dominion and every name that is named not only in this age but also in the one to come, and he put all things in subjection under his feet and* **gave him as head over all things to the church***"* (Ephesians 1:19-22).

The crucified, resurrected, ascended and now glorified Christ returned to the upper room. Meanwhile, his disciples were debating whether or not what they had heard from Mary could possibly be true. Jesus walked through a locked door and into their midst. Then what happened? The disciples freaked out, just as you and I would have done. But Jesus immediately spoke to their fears. He told them to calm down. Be at peace, he said, and showed them his hands and side.

We might wonder if Jesus couldn't have walked through that door before his death and resurrection. After all, he was God. But the fact of the matter is that there is no record that he did. The Scriptures make it plain that he put on human flesh and humbled himself to become a man. He was tempted in all things, yet without sin. He ate and drank with his friends. He got tired and hungry. He walked over dusty roads. Of course, we would never limit the Lord Jesus, but when he showed up suddenly in the midst of those who knew him best, they were certainly shocked. Something truly divine had happened to their beloved Lord.

Once they realized it was he, they really got excited. Pandemonium broke out. Can you imagine the scene? Surely they were grabbing the Lord and taking turns giving him big hugs, just as Mary had in the garden. I'm sure there was a lot of apologizing and asking for forgiveness going on. Undoubtedly, some were saying, "I knew you would be back, I knew it couldn't end like that." Remember, these were emotional disciples who had just gone from the depths of experiencing incredible loss and fear to having their Lord and God returned to them. They loved this man. John says that they rejoiced. We can only imagine.

But what did Jesus do next? Did he tell them to stop clinging to him because he had not yet ascended to his Father? That's what he had earlier said to Mary.

No! On the contrary, he said, *"Peace is with you. As the Father has sent me, I also send you."* Then he breathed into them and said, *"Receive the Holy Spirit. If you forgive the sins of any, they will be forgiven them; if you retain the sins of any, they have been retained."* Both problems solved. Man can receive the divine Spirit and sins can be forgiven.

Remember what was said back at the feast about receiving the living water: *"This he spoke of the Spirit, but the Spirit was not yet given because Jesus was not yet glorified."* Now that Jesus had been resurrected and glorified in his Father's presence, he was able to dispense his life as Spirit into his disciples. The Spirit could be given because Jesus had been glorified. Now those who are thirsting for real life, wherever they are, whenever they live, can receive the Lord Jesus himself, in Spirit, into them. This is tremendous news.

Historically, God—the Father, Son and Spirit—had been involved with man in an external way. Throughout the Old Testament record we see God guiding his people, through the burning bush, through the Shekinah glory, through the Urim and the Thummin in the Holy of Holies and through the rock, fire and cloud in the wilderness, just to cite a few examples.

Now God the Father, Son and Spirit would become one with those who would believe, actually dwelling in them. Jesus made this plain in John 17: 20-23, when he prayed, *"I do not ask on behalf of these alone, but for those also who believe in me through their word, that they may all be one; as you, Father, are in me, and I in You, that they also may be in us so that the world may believe that You sent me. The glory which You have given me I have given to them; that they may be one, just as we are one; I in them, and You in me, that they may be perfected in unity, that the world may know that You have sent me, and have loved them even as You have loved me."* What an amazing fact!

Paul said it this way in Corinthians 12:13: *"For by one Spirit we were all baptized into one body, whether Jews or Greeks, whether slaves or free and we were all made to drink of one Spirit."* This was what Jesus was looking forward to as he declared to those Israelites, *"Come to me and drink.*" Throughout the centuries the thirsty have been finding living water at the feet of this glorious Christ. In fact, we were created with this in mind. You and I were designed by God to be able to drink from spiritual realms and glory there in our Lord. Paul put it this way in Philippians 3:3: *"For we are the true circumcision who worship in the Spirit and glory in Christ Jesus and put no confidence in the flesh."*

God's Authority Is in Christ

The Lord spent forty more days with his followers, explaining how life in his kingdom works. Doubtless he told them what it would be like to follow him in Spirit as compared to following him in the flesh. He told them the day would come soon when they would be empowered as the body of Christ with authority by the outward coming of his Spirit on them on the day of Pentecost. Jesus made no secret of where that authority would come from. *"All authority has been given to me in heaven and on earth, go therefore and make disciples of all the nations, baptizing them into the Name of the Father and the Son and the Holy Spirit… and, lo, I am with you always, even unto the end of the age"* (Matthew 28:18).

What incredibly challenging and yet comforting words: *"I am with you always."* The glorified Christ, to whom all authority had been given, would be living in his followers as Spirit, empowering them from within and without to live for him in this world. Christ, the living water that is in our innermost beings, becomes a river of water that springs up out of us and gives real water to a thirsty world.

Paul stated this when he wrote in II Corinthians 3:17, *"Now the Lord is the Spirit, and where the Spirit of the Lord is, there is liberty. But we all with unveiled face, beholding as a mirror the glory of the Lord, are being transformed into the same image, from glory to glory, just as from the Lord, the Spirit."*

The Scriptures show the intimate connection between the Lord Jesus and the Spirit that resides in us. They are one and the same. To have an experience with the Spirit is to have an experience with Christ. To have an experience with Christ is to have an experience in the Spirit. Paul wrote in I Corinthians 6:17, *"The one who joins himself to the Lord is one Spirit with him."* We are joined to our Lord in our spirits. He is in us as Spirit. That is why it is so important that we recover the deep meaning of how to live in Spirit.

The Richness of the Spirit

Paul described the all-inclusiveness of this incredible Spirit when he wrote to the Romans, *"However, you are not in the flesh, but in the Spirit if indeed the Spirit of God dwells in you. But if anyone does not have the Spirit of Christ, he does not belong to him. If Christ is in you though the body is dead because of sin, yet the Spirit is life because of righteousness. But if the Spirit of him who raised Jesus from the dead dwells in you, he who raised Christ Jesus from the dead will give life to your mortal bodies through his Spirit who indwells you"* (Rom 8:9-11). According to this passage the Spirit of God, the Spirit of Christ, Christ, and the Spirit of him who raised Jesus from the dead are all in us. Wow! So how many Spirits are in us?

Only one.

The amazingly wonderful, glorious Lord Jesus as Spirit brought into us the divine life of his Father God. What a Lord! What a Spirit! Is it any wonder that Paul wrote to the Ephesians that *"through him* [Jesus] *we have our access in one Spirit to the Father"*? Jesus is the good shepherd who leads us into his Father's presence, where we can enjoy the riches to be found there—things like love, joy, peace, patience, long-suffering, kindness, goodness, and self-control.

As Paul wrote in Romans 8:14, *"For all who are being led by the Spirit of God, these are sons of God; for you have not received a spirit of slavery leading to fear again, but you have received the Spirit of adoption whereby we cry, Abba, Father (Daddy, Father). The Spirit himself bears witness with our spirit that we are children of God."* Does this not sound like our Lord Jesus? He said to his disciples, *"Fear not."* He said to Mary, *"Go and tell my brothers and sisters that I go to my Father and your Father and my God and your God."*

This wondrous One who calls "Daddy, Father," from deep within us, bearing witness that we are the children of God, is none other than the Lord Jesus himself, living in us in Spirit. Paul reminded the Galatians of this when he said, *"Because you are sons, God has sent forth the Spirit of his Son into our hearts, crying Abba, Father."* Remember Jesus' comforting words to his followers that he would not leave them as orphans, but that he would come to them. Jesus is the One who reunites us with our heavenly Father. If you have the comforting reassurance deep within that you are a child of God, that assurance comes from the Lord Jesus.

The beauty of all this is the uniqueness that we each hold in the Lord's eyes. Each of us is a new creation in Christ, all together making up the body of Christ in all its richness and variety. As Paul wrote in I Corinthians 12:18, *"But now, God has placed the members each one of them in the body just as he desired."* God loves you deeply and has given you a unique relationship with him. As you join with the Spirit within and call out to him, he makes you complete and the body is built up.

When we see these truths, we don't need to shy away from acknowledging that it is Christ who is the Spirit. On the contrary, we welcome him, our Christ and our Lord. As Spirit, Jesus is intimate with us. As Spirit, Jesus is exalted in our midst. As he said in John 15:26, *"When the Helper comes, whom I will send to you from the Father, the Spirit of truth, who proceeds from the Father, he will bear witness of me."* This is why we have the right to exercise discernment regarding activities carried out in the name of the Spirit which have little resemblance to something Christ would do. There are many claims made in the name of the Spirit. When we hear them, we can ask, "Would our Lord behave in such a way?" If not, then neither would the Spirit, for they are one.

When we read the references to the Spirit in the New Testament, it's clear that the first-century believers had a great deal of familiarity with the Lord as Spirit. They felt comfortable talking about the Spirit. They knew they had a spirit and that Christ resided there. They practiced hearing from the Lord in Spirit. They knew that real prayer emanated from the Spirit within them.

Consider this example in Acts 16:6 when Paul traveled to Macedonia: *"They passed through the Phrygian and Galatian region having been forbidden by the Holy Spirit to speak the word in Asia and when they had come to Mysia, they were trying to go into Bithynia and the Spirit of Jesus did not permit them."* Paul and Silas were called by the Lord to go out and plant churches. They were in great need of his guiding hand. They were not allowed by the Holy Spirit to enter Asia. Then they were kept from entering Bithynia by the Spirit of Jesus. Were there two Spirits they were following? Of course not. The Holy Spirit and the Spirit of Jesus are one and the same. Jesus was alive and well in them, leading his sheep as he promised to do by telling them where to go and where not to go. Thank God, he provides the same kind of leadership today as the Spirit within us.

Making It Practical

Following the Spirit is not some kind of hocus-pocus. It can be dramatic. It can also take much perseverance. But following the Spirit is not an emotional roller coaster ride. It does not involve fear. It is not legalistic. To follow the Spirit is to follow Christ. He is the Spirit in us.

There are good lessons for us as the family of God to learn here. When we read a verse that exhorts us to *"keep the unity of the Spirit in the bond of peace,"* as in Ephesians 3, we all agree that this is a value that God highly regards. This is a verse often quoted, and yet in the United States we have thousands of different church denominations. If our unity is in the Spirit, we evidently don't know how to access that Spirit very well, because believers separate themselves from one another every day. The unity of the Spirit is the unity that exists between the Father and the Son. That is a unity that time, death and eternity will never break.

Much of the New Testament was written to encourage us to a deep understanding of how to access spiritual realms and the experience available there. It was written to help us understand how Christ as the Spirit operates in us. As we turn to him in our spirit and welcome his leadership over our lives, his kingdom is built.

Setting Our Minds on the Spirit

Remembering that the Lord Jesus was Spirit before he was flesh will help us relate to him as Spirit. There is a battle involved here. Because our first consciousness was of the material world, we must learn a new way of living. As Paul said to the Colossians, we now learn *"to set our minds on things above, not on the things of this earth."* He exhorted the Romans *"that to set the mind on the flesh is death; but to set your mind on the Spirit is life and peace."* He encouraged the Corinthians that *"[w]e look not at the things which are seen, but at the things which are not seen: for the things which are seen are temporal; but the things which are not seen are eternal"* (2 Corinthians 4:18).

Consider also the fascinating words spoken by the Apostle Peter. The Lord brought him to Caesarea to share the good news that Christ was resurrected. This was a major step forward for Peter to bring the gospel to the Gentile nations. Listen to how he spoke about Jesus: *"We are witnesses of all the things he did both in the land of the Jews and in Jerusalem. They also put him to death by hanging him on a cross. God raised him up on the third day and granted that he be made visible not to all the people but to witnesses who were chosen beforehand by God, to us who ate and drank with him after he arose from the dead."* (Acts 10: 39-41)

God did the first century believers a favor. He granted that Jesus Christ become visible so his disciples could see him for a little while longer. The resurrected, glorified Christ has the ability to be seen or not seen. He has the capacity to be physical or non-physical. He has the ability to move freely between the seen and unseen realms. That is how he can sit on the throne and still be active on earth as head of the church. For the sake of his disciples as they moved from following him in flesh to following him in Spirit, the Lord allowed himself to be seen by them.

Thankfully, Peter was able to make the transition. He got the big picture. Here's what he wrote to the Jews dispersed throughout the Roman Empire: *"For Christ also died for sins once for all, the just for the unjust, in order that he might bring us to God, having been put to death in the flesh but made alive in the Spirit"* (I Peter 3:18). Peter verified that Jesus Christ is now known by us in Spirit.

Here's how Paul described to the Corinthians the transition from following the physical Christ to following the spiritual Christ: *"Therefore from now on we recognize no man according to the flesh, even though we have known Christ according to the flesh, yet now we know him thus no longer"* (II Corinthians 5:16-17).

In the context of the passage, Paul was talking about how the Corinthians were judging one another according to outward accomplishments. But that is no longer how we are to live. He emphasized the point that we knew Christ according to the flesh, but now we know him thus no longer. If they didn't know Christ according to the flesh, how did they know him? If they weren't thinking about the earthly Jesus who did all the miracles and trying to follow his example, how did they know him?

They knew him in Spirit. They knew him as he wanted to be known—as the living, vibrant Spirit. Jesus did not want to be remembered simply as the Jesus who walked around on the earth in the first century. No, he didn't want to be only remembered as the first century Jesus; he wants to be experienced as the twenty-first century Jesus! That happens in the Spirit.

One day we will see Jesus face to face. Our earthly, physical limitations will be lifted. The Lord will descend out of the heavens with a shout, and we will be like him, for we will see him completely as he is. We will be fully transformed. What a glorious day that will be.

Paul described this in I Corinthians 15:42: *"So also is the resurrection of the dead. It is sown perishable; it is raised imperishable; it is sown in dishonor; it is raised in glory: it is sown in weakness; it is raised in power; It is sown a natural body; it is raised a spiritual body. There is a natural body, and there is a spiritual body, and so it is written, the first man Adam became a living soul; the last Adam a life giving Spirit; however the spiritual is not first but the natural; then the spiritual. The first man is of the earth, earthy: the second man is from heaven; As is the earthy, so also are they that are earthy: and as is the heavenly, so also are those who are heavenly, just as we have borne the image of the earthy, we will also bear the image of the heavenly."*

We have a part in seeing that glorious day arrive. God builds his kingdom as we fellowship with him in heavenly realms. We enter those realms through the Spirit. As Paul put it to the Ephesians, *"And he came and preached peace to you who were far away and peace to those who were near for through him we both have our access in one Spirit to the Father. So then you are no longer strangers and aliens but you are fellow citizens with the saints and are of God's household, having been built on the foundation of the apostles and prophets, Christ Jesus himself being the cornerstone in whom the whole building being fitted together is growing into a holy temple in the Lord in whom you also are being built together into a dwelling of God in the Spirit."* (Ephesians 2:17-22)

My friends claim your birthright. If you are a believer, turn to Christ in your spirit and fellowship with him there. Allow him to bring you into your heavenly Father's loving presence. In the process, the Lord Spirit will build you with other members of his body into the very dwelling of God. What an adventure!

Is it easy to follow a Christ we can't see with our physical eyes? No one who has been at it long would say it is. But the reward is certainly worth the cost. Yes, we will need the eyes of our heart to grasp these realities. But, thank God, he is pleased to reveal them to us. As Paul wrote to the Corinthians, *"Things which eye has not seen, and ear has not heard, and which have not entered the heart of man, all that God has prepared for those who love him. For to us God revealed them through the Spirit: for the Spirit searches all things even the depths of God."* (I. Cor. 2:9-10) His plan is not complicated. It may be mysterious, it may be profound, it may not be easy to apprehend. But it's not complicated.

A good place to start is simply to focus on the words of Paul to the Corinthians. *"Now the Lord is the Spirit...."* Now, today, your Lord, who sits on the throne in the heavens, is the Lord who is the Spirit in you. Remember, he is the ladder that joins heaven and earth. Where he is there is freedom. You are free to meet Christ. You are free to fellowship with him. You are free to go into heavenly realms and fellowship with your majestic Father in the Spirit. This was made possible because the Christ who lived in the glory of God before time began, and who walked on the earth as the last Adam, went to the grave and was resurrected as the life-giving Spirit. He is the Spirit within us. He is our source of forgiveness, of life, of hope, of unity.

One wonderful way to enter into his presence as Spirit is to call out to the Lord. As Paul reminded the Corinthians in I Corinthians 12:3, *"No one can say Jesus is Lord, except by the Holy Spirit."* As you simply call on the name of the Lord Jesus, you will begin to enjoy the sweetness of his presence.

When you pray, be sensitive to his stirring and speaking within you. When you hear his voice, respond with faith. If you are not sure about something you think the Lord is speaking to you about, talk it over with trusted Christian friends. There is safety in the fellowship of the body of Christ. When you need the Lord's guidance in decision making, move away from any sense of darkness and follow the sense of life and peace, for "the mind set on the Spirit is life and peace."

We are reminded in Psalms 100 to *"come before his presence with singing and into his courts with praise."* Singing and praising the Lord are also wonderful ways to move from the wanderings of your mind or the stress of your surroundings into his presence. Paul wrote in Colossians 3:16, *"Let the word of Christ richly dwell within you with all wisdom teaching and admonishing one another with psalms and hymns and spiritual songs, singing with thankfulness in your hearts to God."*

Jesus Christ is alive in his followers as the Holy Spirit. He leads us into fellowship with his Father and into unity with one another. In the process we are made into a dwelling of God in the Spirit through which the nations can see the glory of God and come to their Savior. This move of God began in Jerusalem with the activity of the resurrected and glorified Christ among his people. It continues today wherever God's people are led by this glorious Spirit.

We have been called to be part of this great adventure. Will you take some time today to stop and ask the Lord to show you your place in it? When you hear the word "Spirit" used in Christian circles, be reminded that this mighty Spirit is Christ himself and that he lives in you in your spirit. Remember that as a believer in Christ, made alive by his presence in you, you are more than just body and soul. You have been born from above and now have access to the spiritual realms where God is found. It's time to replace any confusion you once held about the Holy Spirit with a daily, living

85

relationship with the Lord Spirit, Jesus Christ. Turn to him in your spirit and touch him there. He will lead you into all truth.

The Church

"That he might present to himself the Church..." **Ephesians 5:27**

When we come to the subject of the church, we arrive at a great battle ground. We come to the heart of God and the heart of the mystery. As Paul wrote to the Ephesians, *"For Christ loved the church and gave himself up for her."* And again, *"this mystery (of oneness) is great but I am speaking of Christ and the church."* We should not be surprised that such important ground is fiercely contested by God's enemy. The Lord said in Matthew 16, *"I will build my church and the gates of Hell shall not overpower it."* Thank God, we know in advance that in Christ we are on the winning side. But the Lord has enlisted those who believe in him in this epic struggle. Are you ready to follow your Lord into battle to recover the true meaning and experience of the church?

To most Christians worldwide, the word "church" brings to mind a building where Christians with matching views about God gather on Sunday mornings. When first meeting, Christians often ask one another "Where do you go to church?" They do that because it's a polite conversation starter. If you've been a Christian for a while, you also know that based on what kind of building a person goes to on Sunday, you can generally figure out whether or not that person's relationship with God is similar to yours. Then you can decide at what level you can fellowship together. In this way, such exchanges often separate believers more than they bring them together.

The world has certainly done what it can to add to the confusion. Today we find devil worshippers calling themselves the "church of Satan" and witches using the word "church" to describe their covens. What a travesty—the enemy stealing a holy word! But we don't have to simply accept the status quo or be downhearted. Instead we can work to restore this great word to the exalted position God meant it to have and to unleash the tremendous power behind it.

What Is the Church?

Let's begin with the Biblical perspective of what the church is and work forward from there. The word "church" comes from the Greek word *ecclesia*. This word means "the called-out ones" and carries the connotation of an assembly. In several New Testament passages the church is called the "body of Christ." The church, then, is the assembly of those who have been called out of the world to express the reality of who Christ is. That means that when you see the church as it is meant to be, you see Christ. The church shows to the world who he is and what he looks like. It is the visible expression of the invisible Lord Jesus, acting under his direction.

The church is also referred to as a holy nation, a royal priesthood, a bride, and a gathering community where worship, teaching, breaking of bread, fellowship and prayer take place. It is called a holy temple, the dwelling of God in the Spirit. It is an army called to confront the powers of darkness and to display the nature and wisdom of God on the earth.

The church is also called a mystery. There is something mysterious about how the church functions in the here and now. How can an unseen God lead a group of people? How can Christ who sits in the heavens be the head of the church that resides on the earth? This is a mystery. One of the greatest harms that can be done to the church is to demystify her. Over and over the church has been defined down to a set of principles or organizational structures or traditions. In so doing she has been stripped of her mysterious relationship with Christ the Head, the One who loves to do the spontaneous and who is new every morning.

Too often the Lord's ability to work among his people has been limited by church structures that are old and rigid. The church was never meant to become rigid. For believers to group together and act as one, some organization is needed. Our human bodies are wonders of organization and structure. But there is a life pulsing through them which cannot be denied or always predicted. Likewise, the divine life of Christ must be turned loose in his body if we are to have a rich experience of what church is meant to be.

Can you see the church as the apostle Paul saw her—as the Lord's body, filled with his life, moving forward together under his guidance to defeat his enemy while displaying the fullness of him who is filling all in all? If you can't, its time to catch a fresh vision of what the church really is.

A Problem with Definitions

Modern definitions of this glorious word aren't going to help us much. Webster's Dictionary defines church as "a building for Christian worship" or "a service held in it." That is not the church. The church is not a physical building; it has never been a building; it will never be a building. To confine the church to an earthly building, to tie her to bricks and mortar, is the ultimate act of taking away her mobility, her vitality and the mysterious way in which the Lord leads her.

Am I saying that Christians shouldn't get together in large buildings? No, we have to gather somewhere. That's Biblical. But where we gather is not the church, and our experience of Christ should not begin and end in buildings.

When we look to Christian sources for a better definition, we also run into problems. A leading Bible concordance defines church in this way: "A body of Christians." That is close but still incorrect. The church is not a body of Christians. It is the body of Christ. It is Jesus being expressed. If he is not involved, then whatever you have is not the church. That concordance gives a second definition, that the church is "a body of Christians with the same general creed and under the same ecclesiastical authority." Wrong again. How do you get from the exciting, dynamic and mysterious body of Christ of the

Scriptures to a group of people who agree on some doctrines and are under some kind of ecclesiastical authority? There is nothing man-made about the church. It is born of God and manifests his love for his Son and for all peoples of the earth.

How about the beautiful word *ecclesia*? We see it surface today in the word "ecclesiastic." "Ecclesiastic" is defined in this way: "of or relating to a church as a formal and established institution"; or, "suitable for use in a church, i.e. vestments." Once again, how did we get there from "called out ones"? The church God birthed is not a formal and established institution. It is his body, alive and full of spontaneity. It is not limited by formality. Yes, our church experience should certainly contain awe-filled times of worship; but the extrapolation from there is not to formality and institutionalism. What could be more informal than the disciples lying around on cushions, eating a meal and listening to their Lord? That is the cradle of the church.

We should rue the fact that in our day "ecclesiastic" has been defined down to refer to vestments, or "articles of ceremonial attire and insignia worn by ecclesiastic officials as indicative of their rank." Even reading that aloud makes the air stuffy. Where did Christianity go wrong? To load the church down with rank and insignia or to define it down into creeds and traditions restricts its living dynamism.

Is there rank in the church? Well, there are apostles and prophets and pastors and teachers and gifts of administration and many other roles. But there's no rank. How is honor expressed in the church? According to the apostle Paul, *"those members of the body, which we deem less honorable, on these we bestow more abundant honor; and our unseemly members come to have more abundant seemliness"* (1 Corinthians 12:23). The lesser are to be honored more than the greater. There are different roles, but there's no rank.

It's time for a change. There is a mystery about the way that Christ leads his church that doesn't fit into organizational charts. There's a mystery in the relationship between an invisible Christ who wants to lead and be one with his people through his Spirit and how that expresses itself. Restoring the vitality of the word "church" will take us from the stiffness of ecclesiastic vestments, rank and insignia to the newness of ecclesia. It is a journey worth taking. We may need to leave the familiar. But there is a land flowing with milk and honey waiting on the horizon.

The Gathering Church

Realizing that the church is the assembly of Christ, what is unique—or should be—about Christian gatherings? Is it not the presence of the Lord Jesus, in Spirit, in his people? The church is an assembly of people where the Lord Jesus goes for fellowship. When we gather together, our greatest hope and expectation is that he will be there. And not just there in some ethereal, esoteric sense, but that he will actually be there. We will sense his presence. We will hear his voice. We will experience his love. Sure, we have all been in Christian gatherings where that has not been our experience. But the best way to see the richness, variety and vitality of Christ in a Christian gathering is to turn God's people loose to bring what they have of Christ.

That's why Paul told the Corinthians, *"When you assemble, each one has a psalm, has a teaching, has a revelation, has a language, has an interpretation. Let all things be done for edification."* (I Cor. 14:26) Now that sounds like a dynamic get-together. Can such freedom cause some problems? It certainly did in Corinth. But Paul's response was to encourage more participation, not less. Modern-day church practice, however, has turned meeting control into an art form. We need to head back in Paul's direction if we want to experience the life God has in mind for his church.

The opportunity to see something great of Christ is going to increase appreciably where people have the freedom to come to meetings and offer something of Christ to the gathering. There will be richness there because Christ is expressing himself through his body. And yes, there will be order. If Christ is truly leading, then the One in charge is he who gave order to the universe and who still holds it together. Will there also be spontaneity? Yes, because, as C.S. Lewis wrote, "He is not a tame lion."

The Old Testament Sanctuary

There is a rich picture of this in the Old Testament that helps us understand what the real purpose of church, of ecclesia, is. That picture can be seen in the tabernacle. The Old Testament tabernacle was also called the tent of meeting. It was the place God used to dwell among his people and speak with them. God called it his sanctuary.

Here is how God introduced his people to this special place: *"Then the LORD spoke to Moses, saying, Tell the sons of Israel to raise a contribution for Me, from every man whose heart moves him you shall raise my contribution…And let them construct a sanctuary for me; that I may dwell among them"* (Exodus 25:1, 8). Once the tabernacle was built with those contributions of gold, silver, bronze, fine linen and so on, the Israelites continued to bring their offerings there, and God met with them. This is described in Exodus 29:42: *"It shall be a continual burnt offering throughout your generations at the doorway of the tent of meeting before the LORD: where I will meet with you, to speak to you there."*

The Lord's purpose in having the tabernacle set up was two directional: God would have a place on the earth to come where he could meet with his people and speak to them. God's people would have a place where they could go to hear from their God and where they could bring something that satisfied him.

Before the tabernacle was built, the Lord had already given Moses the Ten Commandments, the requirements for living in relationship with a holy God. Those commandments, written on tablets, were put in a box called the Ark of the Covenant in the inner chamber of the tabernacle. That inner chamber was called the Holy of Holies. It was there that God's presence dwelt. The Israelites were given the written requirements for living with God, but that was not to be the totality of his interaction with them. He wanted them to live by his direct instructions! Even though God gave them the Ten Commandments as a reflection of who he was and what it would take to live successfully in his presence, he also wanted to directly relate to them through the tabernacle. Notice his words, *"There I will meet with you…I will speak to you about all that I will give you in commandment for the sons of Israel"* (Exodus 25:22). This is the

God we have. He has always wanted to be in direct relationship with those he created and loves.

The tabernacle was the place where the people of God brought their offerings. These offerings were taken to a certain place. Do you know where that place was? Over and over again in Exodus and Leviticus we read that the people were to bring their offerings to the door of the tabernacle. They were also to congregate there when the Lord had something to say to them. The door holds special significance for us in this regard. The burnt offerings (Exodus 40:6), the sin offerings (Leviticus 7:2), the peace offerings (Numbers 6:18), the guilt offerings (Leviticus 19:21) and the grain offerings (Exodus 29:41) were all to be brought to the door of the tabernacle for presentation to the priests and through them to God.

Standing at the Door

Consider these fascinating verses in Exodus 33:7-11: *"Now Moses used to take the tent and pitch it outside the camp, a good distance from the camp, and he called it the tent of meeting. And everyone who sought the LORD would go out to the tent of meeting which was outside the camp And it came about, whenever Moses went out to the tent, that all the people would arise and stand, each at the entrance of his tent, and gaze after Moses until he entered the tent. Whenever Moses entered the tent, the pillar of cloud would descend and stand at the entrance of the tent; and the LORD would speak with Moses. When all the people saw the pillar of cloud standing at the entrance of the tent, all the people would arise and worship each at the entrance of his tent. Thus the LORD used to speak to Moses face to face, just as a man speaks to his friend."*

At the time this tent of meeting was set up, the Lord was very angry with the Israelites. While Moses was up on the mountain getting instructions from God on how to live as a people set apart for him, the Israelites got impatient, not knowing what Moses was up to or if he was even still alive. Believing they needed some kind of god for protection, they foolishly demanded that Aaron make them one. Gathering together golden earrings, he had a golden calf constructed. Naturally, when Moses came down out of the presence of the living God, he was furious with the people. He had the calf demolished and God caused a plague to fall on the idolatrous people. Nonetheless, God still wanted to dwell among his people. So Moses took this tent and set it up outside the camp and called it the tent of meeting.

Everyone who sought the Lord would go out to the tent of meeting. God made himself available to them there. This is what made the Israelites unique in all the earth. God didn't interact with the Philistines or the Canaanites or the Amalekites or the Amorites or any of the other people dwelling in that area. He dwelt with the Israelites and his place of dwelling among them was the sanctuary, the tent of meeting.

Moses and his servant Joshua were the only ones who went into the tent. When Moses went out to that tent, all of the Israelites watched him go. Not only that, whenever Moses went out to the tent, all the men would also go somewhere. They went to the doorway of their own tents. In the culture of the day, the man represented his whole household, so this picture represents all of God's people. The men would arise and stand at the door of their tents. Whenever Moses entered the tent, a cloud came down and God would come to meet and speak with Moses. What an experience! Picture your God, waiting for Moses to come out to the tent so he could meet with him and they could just talk, face to face as a man would talk to his friend. Meanwhile, all the men of Israel would arise and worship, each at the doorway to his tent. The whole nation of Israel was involved in this picture of God having fellowship with his people.

At that time Moses went in and met with God face to face. But can you see the symbolism as all those men stood in their doorways, worshipping as well, probably wondering what it was like, and wishing they, too, could be like Moses, spending time with God as they would with a friend? It sounds like a comfortable encounter. What an incredible picture of the importance of the sanctuary that was the tent of meeting.

But does that have something to do with the church? Yes! The day has come when all the people of God can enter that tent of meeting and know him, face to face, and talk with him as a man talks with his friend. Here's how the apostle John described meeting with the living God: *"What was from the beginning, what we have heard, what we have seen with our eyes, what we beheld and our hands handled, concerning the Word of Life, and the life was manifested, and we have seen and bear witness and proclaim to you the eternal life, which was with the Father and was manifested to us, what we have seen and heard we proclaim to you also, so that you also may have fellowship with us; and indeed our fellowship is with the Father, and with his Son Jesus Christ."* (I John 1: 1-3) That is very personal! Thank God, we, too, have been invited into the tent of meeting to fellowship with the Father and the Son.

Paul said the same thing when he wrote, *"God is faithful, through whom you were called into fellowship with his Son, Jesus Christ our Lord"* (I Corinthians 1:9). He made it clear that all God's people were included in this wonderful fellowship when he said, *"For you are all sons of God through faith in Christ Jesus. For all of you who were baptized into Christ have clothed yourselves with Christ. There is neither Jew nor Greek, there is neither slave nor free man, there is neither male nor female; for you are all one in Christ Jesus"* (Galatians 3:26-28).

The church is the corporate body of God's people living lives in fellowship with him. It's the place where God dwells with his people and where he gives them direction. Today we, as believers in Christ, can go through him to have fellowship with our God. We have the kind of access that the High Priest of the tabernacle could only have dreamed about. The High Priest could only enter into the copy of the true tabernacle. We enter into our heavenly Father's very presence. When we assemble together, we can share the riches that we have found in fellowship with our Lord and through his activity in our lives. That will include real-life struggles, victories, prayers, praises, sorrows and songs. Encouraged by the realness of Christ in our midst, we can then go out to declare the excellences of a loving God to a world in darkness. This is the mission of the church.

When God first brought the Israelites out of Egypt, he wanted a whole nation of priests. Exodus 19:5 says, *"Now then, if you will indeed obey my voice and keep my covenant, then you shall be my own possession among all the peoples…and you shall be to me a kingdom of priests and a holy nation."* But under the old covenant God singled out one family (Aaron's) of the tribe of Levi to carry out the duties of the priesthood. Out of that tribe only the High Priest could actually enter the Holy of Holies where God dwelt. Jesus Christ changed all that. He did not come from the tribe of Levi but from the tribe of Judah. He was the first of a new order of priests. As Peter wrote in his first letter to the church scattered across Asia, *"And coming to him as to a living stone which has been rejected by men, but choice and precious in the sight of God, you also, as living stones,* **are being built up as a spiritual house for a holy priesthood***, to offer up spiritual sacrifices acceptable to God through Jesus Christ… you are a chosen race,* **a royal priesthood,** *a holy nation, a people for God's own possession, so that you may proclaim the excellencies of him who has called you out of darkness into his marvelous light."* (I Peter 2:4, 11)

The church was not designed to be an assembly of people where just one or a few people who have been in the presence of God describe what that is like while everyone else watches and worships as best they can. If that is all we have we are much like those Israelites standing at their tents hoping Moses was enjoying his time with God. The New Testament church is a body of people who all fellowship with God, proclaim how great he is and collectively express his will on the earth. This takes many forms including meeting for worship, reaching out to the poor, praying for one another, caring for the sick, gathering for teaching, being a witness in our jobs and communities and so forth. That is powerful!

Everyone Plays a Part

The reality of the church being a corporate people expressing the richness of God's goodness is reinforced in other Old Testament passages. We have already cited God's instructions for how the tabernacle was to be built where Exodus 25 says, *"from every man whose heart moves him you shall raise my contribution."* Everyone with a willing heart was asked to contribute. Everyone had something they could give.

Consider these verses:

Exodus 35:5: *"Take from among you a contribution to the LORD; whoever is of a willing heart, let him bring it as the LORD'S contribution: gold, silver, and bronze."*

Exodus 35:29: *"The Israelites, all the men and women, whose heart moved them to bring material for all the work, which the LORD had commanded through Moses to be done, brought a freewill offering to the LORD."*

Exodus 36:5: *"and they said to Moses, 'The people are bringing much more than enough for the construction work which the LORD commanded us to perform.'"*

These contributions all related to a physical, earthly building. Today, God's church is more than buildings made with human hands. That's why the writer of Hebrews wrote of the Old Testament saints, *"And all these, having gained approval through their faith, did not receive what was promised, because God had provided something better for us, so that apart from us they would not be made perfect"* (Hebrews 11:39-40). God builds his church by stirring up the hearts of those who love him to offer what they can to build up his body. When he does that, there is more than enough to accomplish what God wants.

Sadly, we often consider the work of the church to be what is done by those in "full-time Christian service." Because of this, many of God's people have been content with a seat on the sidelines watching and evaluating the performance of others. This was never the way the church was supposed to express its vitality. Paul laid that out in Ephesians 4:11-12: *"He gave some as apostles, and some as prophets, and some as evangelists, and some as pastors and teachers, for the equipping of the saints for the work of service, to the building up of the body of Christ."* This verse says that while certain gifted ones give tools to the greater body of Christ (the saints, the holy ones), we are all to be involved in the work of building up the body. Most of us are very familiar with these verses but have not actually seen them played out in our experience of church.

We need those who share the wonders of Christ and the greatness of his plan with the people of God. But as Paul said in verses 15 and 16, *"we are to grow up in all aspects into him who is the head, even Christ, from whom the whole body, being fitted and held together by that which every joint supplies, according to the proper working of each individual part, causes the growth of the body for the building up of itself in love."* This is the whole body of Christ energized by his life flow, giving what they have, working together and falling in love with one another and their Lord in the process. What a worthy goal! God has given his people the gifts needed to see the building built. To the extent that we can impact the practice of the church, let's help turn them loose.

The Tabernacle Moves into the House

The tabernacle was God's dwelling place among his people as they moved across the wilderness. But when they got into the Promised Land, that arrangement changed. God established a permanent place where his Name would dwell and where the Israelites would come to gather before him. Here's what Deuteronomy 12:5-6 says: *"But you shall seek the Lord at the place which the LORD your God shall choose to establish his name there for his dwelling, and there shall you come: And there you shall bring your burnt offerings, your sacrifices, your tithes, the contribution of your hand, and your vows, and your freewill offerings, and the first born of your herds and of your flocks."*

II Chronicles 6:6 shows where this place is: *"But I have chosen Jerusalem that my name might be there."* When the Israelites entered the Promised Land, Jerusalem was established as the place where God's Name would be honored and the temple, the house of God, was built to be God's sanctuary. II Chronicles 7:1 describes what happened when the temple was finished: *"Now when Solomon had finished praying, fire came down from heaven, and consumed the burnt offering and the sacrifices; and the glory of the Lord filled the house. And the priests could not enter into the house of the Lord, because the glory of the Lord had filled the Lord's house."*

As God's plan moved from the temporary to the permanent in the Old Testament, the tabernacle became the temple. The temple was referred to most often as the house of God. The amazing thing is that God actually filled that house with his presence and glory. There was a place on earth, in Jerusalem, where God dwelt and from which he wanted to lead his people.

The apostles Paul and Peter also refer to the New Testament church as the house of God. This is the place on earth where God's presence and glory is most clearly seen. While the term "house of God" is commonly used in our day to refer to a building where religious people gather, in God's mind his house is not a building made of brick or stone but one of living stones filled with the Lord Jesus. As Paul wrote to the Corinthians, *"For we are God's fellow workers; you are God's field, God's building"* (I Corinthians 3:9).

The Tabernacle Becomes Real

When the Lord Jesus arrived on earth, he came as the true tabernacle of God. John described his coming in this way: *"The Word became flesh and dwelt* (literally, tabernacled) *among us; and we beheld his glory, glory as of the only begotten from the Father, full of grace and truth"* (John 1:14). When Jesus Christ came to earth, the beginning of God's plan to fully indwell his creation became a reality.

One day Jesus walked with his disciples past the temple in Jerusalem. His disciples were impressed. "Wow, what a building, what an incredible temple!" they said. Jesus' response was amazing: *"Tear this temple down and in three days I will raise it again."* We know that he was speaking of the temple which was his body. He was the real house of God come to earth!

But was that the fullness of God's plan? No, there is more to the story. Jesus Christ was crucified, resurrected, glorified, and then returned to his disciples and breathed his Spirit into them in the upper room. Then on Pentecost, the Holy Spirit anointed all the followers of Christ and the ecclesia, the church, the body of Christ, was fully born.

Let's consider what's happening. In the Old Testament the temporary tabernacle expanded into the temple. But these were only copies or pictures of what was to come. In the New Testament the tabernacling Christ, limited by human flesh, expanded into the house of God by indwelling believers with his Holy Spirit. That's what Peter was talking about when he wrote in I Peter 2:4, *"Coming to Jesus as to a living stone, rejected by men, but choice and precious in the sight of God, you also, as living stones, are being built up as a spiritual house, for a holy priesthood, to offer up spiritual sacrifices, acceptable to God through Jesus Christ."*

Paul echoed this in Ephesians 2:20-22 where he wrote, *"Christ Jesus himself being the chief corner stone; in whom the whole building being fitly framed together is growing into a holy temple in the Lord: In whom you also are being built together into a dwelling of God in the Spirit."* This is the church, vital, alive and growing into a dwelling of God in the Spirit. This is the church that you and I joined when we became followers of the Lord Jesus.

The Source of Life

How does this church get built? From where does it derive its energy, its direction and its unity? The answer is clear from our Old Testament pictures. God dwelt in the Holy of Holies in the tabernacle and the temple. From there he gave direction to his people. But only one high priest could go in there, and that was once a year. The best an Israelite in the wilderness could do was stand at his tent door and watch while Moses fellowshipped with God. The best an Israelite in the Promised Land could do was go to Jerusalem three times a year and bring an offering to the priest.

But where is the Holy of Holies today? It is still in the heart of the temple. We who are believers in Christ are the temple! In each of us there is a sacred place called our spirit where Christ dwells. The writer of Hebrews put it this way in Hebrews 10:10: *"By this will, we have been sanctified through the offering of the body of Jesus Christ once for all."* And again in verse 14, *"For by one offering he has perfected for all time those that are sanctified."* The word "sanctified" is a very important one. This is the same word from which the word "sanctuary" comes. There is a connection between the sanctuary and our being sanctified. We have been set apart, called out from the kingdom of darkness, to be the sanctuary of the living God, to be his dwelling place. That is glorious!

This is what the Lord Jesus was talking about in John 17:22-23 when he said, *"The glory which you have given me, I have given to them, that they may be one, just as we are one, I in them and you in Me that they may be perfected in unity."* Through our fellowship with the Christ within us, we enter the presence of our God and Father. He is in us and we are in him. As we individually and corporately fellowship with him and follow his voice, he builds us together into his very dwelling. That's a church we could live and die for.

Paul wrote to the Corinthians, *"Don't you know that you are a sanctuary of God and the spirit of God dwells in you?"* (1 Corinthians 3:16). Who would you rather be, one of those Israelites standing at their tent door worshipping and wishing they could know what was going on in there with Moses, or a believer in the twenty-first century who can go into your inner room and fellowship with your loving Father? He is in us to speak to us, to meet with us, to fellowship with us, to love us, to talk to us face to face as we talk to a friend. This is the life blood of ecclesia. This is the source and well-spring of the church. Thank God, the Old Testament pictures are gone and the reality has come.

Three Aspects of the Church

The Bible describes the church in three ways. There is the church local. That is the fellowship of believers found in a specific geographical location. Paul refers to the "church of God which is at Corinth," "the churches of Galatia," "the church of the Thessalonians," and so forth. That church could meet in homes, as they did in the home of Nymphas in Laodicea, the house of Philemon in Colosse, and the home of Priscilla and Aquila in Rome. Or it could meet at a central place like Solomon's Porch in Jerusalem. The point is that all of the believers in a location were part of the same church, the same body of Christ. Did they all meet together all the time? Not necessarily. Were all the meetings the same? Not likely. Surely they met for teaching, for meals, for prayer, and for fellowship. But wherever they met and however they met, all the believers were still part of the same church.

In part, due to our denominationalism, we have lost a sense of connection to the whole body of Christ in our geographic areas. While most churches are not likely to surrender their denominational names, it would be healthier if we would at least identify ourselves as the part of the church that we are drawn to rather than as the whole church itself. It's not likely we'll ever see signs reading "The First Baptist Part of the Church in Scranton," or "the United Congregational Part of the Church in Des Moines," or the "Holy Spirit Revival Part of the Church in Los Angeles." But if it were done, those doing it would be acknowledging that the believers who live in a city are all part of a larger body, working to see God's will carried out in their location.

Secondly there is the church universal. This is the body of Christ spread all over the world, through which the Lord is doing his kingdom work. It is a great encouragement to be aware of, and in some measure connected to, the work God is doing around the world. It is especially important that we in the West, who experience little of suffering or opposition for our faith, have some idea of what our fellow believers are suffering for the Name of Christ in foreign lands. Such knowledge is both humbling and stirring.

Thirdly, there is the church timeless. This is the body of Christ across the ages, saved by the blood of the Lamb, made up of all those whose names are recorded in the Lamb's book of Life. This is the church referred to by Paul in Ephesians 5:25-27 when he wrote, *"Husbands, love your wives, just as Christ also loved the church, and gave himself up for her; That he might sanctify her having cleansed her by the washing of water by the word, That he might present to himself the church in all her glory, having no spot, or wrinkle, or any such thing; but that she should be holy and blameless."*

We see that church, that glorious assembly of God's people, again in Revelation 21:2 where the apostle John writes, *"And I saw the holy city, new Jerusalem, coming down out of heaven from God, made ready as a bride adorned for her husband."* Now pay attention to the next verse: *"And I heard a loud voice from the throne saying, Behold, the tabernacle of God is among men, and he shall dwell among them, and they shall be his people, and God himself shall be among them."*

This is the ultimate purpose of God in this universe: to dwell with and in his people. He wants us to have a foretaste of that holy city now through the body of Christ, the church. It is through the church that the Lord makes his wisdom known; it is through the church that he defeats his enemy. It is through the church that the nations catch a glimpse of the greatness of our God. Our challenge is to practice and encourage the free movement of Christ in his people so that more of him can be expressed on this earth and his enemy can be crushed.

When you hear the word "church," remind yourself that the church is not a physical building but a vibrant body of people who follow Christ together. Remember that church is not something that can be experienced only on Sundays but happens when the Lord's people are linked together in the love of God and unite to express his will on the earth. The Lord said, "I will build my church and the gates of hell will not overpower it." In that light, let's ask the Lord to work anew in his church to bring beauty, vitality and newness to his people. In this way the earth will be blessed and many will come to the light of his presence. It is the Lord who must build if we are to have newness in our relationship with him and other believers. But he has invited us to labor with him as the object of his affection, his body, the church. We are the glorious apple of his eye and his partner in defeating our common foe. May it be so in our experience.

The Name of the Lord

"Whatever you do in word or deed,

do all in the name of the Lord Jesus" **Colossians 3:17**

It would be hard to imagine a name more loved worldwide than the name of Jesus Christ. At the same time, there is not a name more maligned. Undoubtedly millions around the world love the name of the Lord. Many suffer severe persecution rather than disown it. Yet millions more use this name as a daily curse without giving it a second thought. There's no counting how many times the Lord's name is uttered in frustration and anger when things go poorly.

Why would this be so? Wouldn't it make more sense when something awful happens to curse the name of some mass murderer like Hitler or Stalin or the name of Satan, the ultimate hater of mankind? But that isn't the way it works. Let's consider what Jesus did to have his name treated with such disdain. He revealed a loving God to mankind, spoke on behalf of the oppressed, healed the sick, performed miracles, gave hope to the hopeless and ultimately sacrificed his own life for the sake of others. Those are all reasons for worship, not disdain. The obvious explanation is that God's enemy, whose lying influence permeates this present age, wants this Name to be dishonored and trivialized above all others. But, thank God, in his eternal plan, the centuries-long effort to ridicule and stain the name of the Lord Jesus will fail.

What is your experience like with the name of the Lord? Is it a daily place of retreat where you find strength, solace and security as Solomon described in Proverbs 18:10, *"The name of the Lord is a strong tower, the righteous runs into it and is safe"*? If so, you are truly blessed.

If your experience with the name of the Lord is less than that, or if you have the sense that there are depths to the Lord's name that you have not yet discovered, then this chapter was written with you in mind. It was written to bring you into a deeper relationship with your Lord and to unleash the power of this name into your life. If, for you, "in the name of the Lord" or "in your name" have become phrases tacked onto the end of prayers or spoken as a type of salutation over God's people that have very little practical effect on your life, be assured that Paul had much more than that in mind when he wrote to the Colossians, *"Whatever you do in word or deed, do all in the name of the Lord Jesus."* That is an amazing charge. In the Old Testament, God's special name was Jehovah, revealed to the ancient Hebrews in Exodus 6:2 when God said, *"I am the LORD."* This name was never pronounced except by the high priest on the great Day of Atonement when he entered into the Holy of Holies. How wonderful that today the Almighty God has a name by which we can call him and within whose jurisdiction we can live out our lives. That name is Jesus. Thanks to him, every day for us is a day of atonement.

The Authority of the Lord's Name

Like a beautiful diamond, there are many angles from which the Lord's Name can be examined and admired. In this book we will first consider the authority inherent in the Lord's name itself. Then we'll look at what it means to act in the authority of that name. Paul described the authority inherent in the Lord's name in this way: *"Therefore…God bestowed on him the Name that is above every Name, that at the Name of Jesus, every knee should bow of those who are in heaven and on earth and under the earth and that every tongue should confess that Jesus Christ is Lord, to the glory of God the Father"* (Philippians 2:9-11). Because the Lord Jesus was willing to obey his Father and give himself up to death on behalf of a sinful humanity that his Father loved and wanted a relationship with, the Name of Jesus carries an honor above all others. One day every tongue will confess his Lordship. But we can experience its benefits today. When we do, a beautiful door of fellowship opens between us and our God.

This was the practice in the churches that the apostle Paul planted. Listen to how he opened his letter to the Corinthians: *"Paul…to the church of God which is at Corinth, to those that have been sanctified in Christ Jesus, saints by calling, with all who in every place call upon the name of our Lord Jesus Christ, their Lord and ours."* These verses indicate that Paul had previously taught the believers in all the churches to call on the Lord; to have his Name, "Lord Jesus," on their lips. Why? Because, as Peter preached in Jerusalem, *"There is salvation in no one else for there is no other name under heaven that has been given among men by which we must be saved"* (Acts 4:12).

It's no wonder that God's enemy wants the Name of Jesus to be disdained and trivialized. The power of salvation is available in this name. God has always meant for it to be this way. On Pentecost, Peter made this clear when he quoted the Old Testament prophet Joel in declaring to the crowd, *"And it shall be that everyone who calls on the name of the Lord shall be saved"* (Acts 2:21). How does that work? When we first invited the Lord to come and dwell in us, he made our spirits alive. When we subsequently call on him, we come in contact with that spirit, where Christ our Savior now resides.

The apostle Paul helps us understand this in the letter he wrote to the Corinthians. Here is how he put it in chapter 12, v. 3: *"Therefore I make known to you that no one speaking by the Spirit of God says, 'Jesus is accursed,' and no one can say Jesus is Lord except by the Holy Spirit."* You can access the riches found in spiritual realms by confessing the Lordship of Jesus. Paul says the same thing to the Romans when he writes, *"The word is near you, in your mouth, and in your heart: that is, the word of faith, which we are preaching, that if you confess with your mouth Jesus, Lord and believe in your heart that God raised him from the dead, you shall be saved; for with the heart man believes, resulting in righteousness; and with the mouth he confesses, resulting in salvation… for the same Lord is Lord of all abounding in riches for all that call upon him, for whoever will call on the name of the Lord will be saved."* (Romans 10:8-12)

Peter knew it. Paul knew it. Now it's your turn to discover what they knew to be true: there are riches waiting for you in learning to call on the name of the Lord. Confessing his name, and putting yourself under his Lordship, opens those riches to you. This is not some type of mantra or a nervous placing of the word "Lord" in every other word of your prayers, but a sincere turning to the One who is greater than you are and allowing him access to your life.

There are over a hundred references in the Psalms to the greatness of the Lord's Name. Here are just a few of them:

Psalm 80:18: *"Then we shall not turn back from you; Revive us, and we will call upon your name."*

Psalm 99:6: *"Moses and Aaron were among his priests, and Samuel was among those who called on his name; they called upon the Lord and he answered."*

Psalm 105:1: *"Oh give thanks to the Lord, call upon his name; Make known his deeds among the peoples."*

Psalm 116:4: *"Then I called upon the name of the Lord: 'O Lord, I beseech you, save my life!'"*

Psalm 116:13: *"I shall lift up the cup of salvation and call upon the name of the Lord."*

Psalm 116:17: *"To you I shall offer a sacrifice of thanksgiving, and call upon the name of the Lord."*

Psalm 124:8: *"Our help is in the name of the Lord, Who made heaven and earth."*

Paul encouraged Timothy to do the same when he wrote, *"flee from youthful lusts and pursue righteousness, faith, love and peace, with those who call on the Lord from a pure heart"* (II Timothy 2:22). God has given us a new heart made pure by the shed blood of Jesus Christ and sanctified by his presence. Now he wants to fill that heart with his life. Out of that pure heart and the love that he has placed there, nothing makes more sense than to turn to Jesus and call on his name.

Doing All in the Name

We have taken a Biblical look at the authority in the Lord's name and the benefits of calling on him. Now let's consider what it might mean to do all things in the authority of his name. There are two things we should realize before we head too far down this road. The first is that doing all things in his name does not mean that we are responsible or able to do everything as Jesus did. It does not mean that God is expecting us to be super Christians who do great works for God and live in sinless perfection, obeying his every command. Far from it. That exalted place belongs to only one person, the Lord Jesus himself. Only as we find ourselves in him, living by the power that he provides, can we truly act in his Name. The second thing we should face up to is that simply applying "in your name" to the back end of whatever we are praying does not mean that Jesus has automatically authorized it.

Keep in mind that Paul's exhortation to do all in the name of the Lord Jesus comes at the end of Colossians 3. Paul spent Colossians 1 and 2 making it clear that Jesus Christ is our hope of glory, the head of the church, the mystery of God, the mighty one who lives in our hearts, and the very life by which we live. When we were dead in our sins he made us alive. All of that makes it clear that Christ, not us, is the center of God's universe; he is the one who is going to fill all in all. Keep things in perspective by realizing that whatever it means to do all in the name of the Lord Jesus will bring freedom to us and glory to God. It is not a matter of you "living the victorious Christian life" by your great effort. It's a matter of finding your true resting place in Christ and living from there.

The Name is a Place

Let's take a look at some Old Testament Scriptures that shed more light on the Lord's name.

Here are God's instructions to Moses in Deuteronomy 12:5 as his people were about to enter the Promised Land: *"But you shall seek the Lord at the place where the LORD your God shall choose from all your tribes to put his name there for his dwelling …there also you and your households shall eat before the LORD your God, and rejoice in all your undertakings in which the LORD your God has blessed you…then it shall come about that the place which the LORD your God shall choose for his name to dwell; there shall you bring all that I command you…And you shall rejoice before the LORD your God, you, and your sons and daughters, and your male and female servants…"*

The story of the Israelites coming out of Egypt into the Promised Land is a beautiful picture of how God saved us out of darkness and this present evil age and brought us into the kingdom of his Son. The Israelites were told that when they entered this good land there would be a particular place where God would establish his name. For God to establish his name somewhere is for him to establish his residence there. We can see from this that where God's name is, his presence is also; the two are synonymous.

Previous to this, the Lord made it clear what the Israelites were supposed to do to every other name in that place. Deuteronomy 12:2-3 tell us, *"You shall utterly destroy all the places, where the nations whom you shall dispossess served their gods, on the high mountains, and on the hills, and under every green tree…and you shall cut down the graven images of their gods, and you shall obliterate their name from that place."* They were to obliterate the names of all the previous gods that had defiled the land. Only one name was to be revered in that good land.

This is essentially the same message that Paul presented to the Colossians on a personal and spiritual level. We are not called to physically drive out such nations as the Hittites, the Amorites, and the Canaanites and obliterate their gods like the Israelites of old, but we have our own enemies to obliterate. As Paul wrote in Colossians 3:8, *"But now you also, put them all aside: anger, wrath, malice, slander, and abusive speech from your mouth. Do not lie to one another, since you laid aside the old self with its evil practices… but Christ is all, and in all."* When we get into Christ, there is only to be one name honored there, that is the name of the Lord Jesus, himself.

Everyone Participates

For the Israelites, joy was a result of coming to the place where the Lord's Name dwelt. Here were their instructions: *"and there you shall bring your burnt offerings, your sacrifices, your tithes, the contributions of your hand, and your vows, and your freewill offerings."* When they brought everything together, they ate before the Lord and had a great feast. In today's vernacular, they had a big party. They rejoiced, and everyone, down to the servants, was involved. When we act in the Lord's name we should also experience blessing. That is because we will be in relationship with Jesus, who loves us passionately!

Paul told the Colossians, *"Therefore let no one act as your judge in regard to food or drink or in respect to a festival or a new moon or a Sabbath day, things which are a mere shadow of what is to come; but the substance belongs to Christ"* (Colossians 2:16). Paul tells us something wonderful here. Christ is the reality of the Old Testament festivals. The scene that Moses described in Deuteronomy 12 found its fulfillment in Christ. While those festivals represented far more than simply feasting, the fact is that if you dwell in Christ, you're abiding in a place where joyous celebrations are part of the experience. You're going to have a feast, and that feast is Christ.

Doing all in the Lord's Name will not make you an uptight, legalistic, religious bigot as our modern culture tries to stereotype Christians. It sets you free. As the apostle Paul put it, *"Where the Spirit of the Lord is, there is liberty"* (II Corinthians 3:17).

Consider these verses in Deuteronomy 14:23: *"You shall eat in the presence of the LORD your God, at the place where he chooses to establish his name...in order that you may learn to fear the LORD your God always. If the distance is so great for you that you are not able to bring your offering... then you shall exchange it for money, and take the money in your hand and go to the place which the LORD your God chooses. You may spend the money for whatever your heart desires: for oxen, or sheep, or wine, or strong drink, or whatever your heart desires; and there you shall eat in the presence of the LORD your God and rejoice, you and your household."*

Notice that this place where they were to bring their offerings was the place that God chose to establish his name. That was the place of his presence. The Israelites were required to go there. If their offering was so heavy they couldn't carry it all, then they were to sell it, take the money and go. But they had to go to the place where God set his name, where his name dwelt. It's wonderful that they could buy whatever their heart desired. Their offering came out of a free will, and they had a part in choosing it. They could bring whatever came out of the fullness and the richness of their hearts. Everything that land produced was good and could be brought to God as an offering. When they got there, they would eat with their household in the presence of the Lord God and rejoice.

This all has meaning for our Christian experience. We begin our Christian lives by receiving the Lord Jesus. He is the good land from which we get our life, our sustenance, our security and our future. By calling on his Name, we enter into him, the very place of the divine presence of our God and Father. Paul put it this way in Colossians 2:9: *"for in him* [Christ] *all the fullness of Deity dwells in bodily form."* As we draw on his life, we enjoy the fruits that we find in his Spirit: love, joy, peace, patience, kindness, goodness, faithfulness, gentleness and self control. Real life is found when we experience the benefits of all that is ours in Christ. That is what it means to reap the benefits of living in his wonderful Name. As Paul succinctly put it, *"For me to live is Christ."* Christ becomes the source of our actions. That is an offering pleasing to God and beneficial to us.

This picture is reinforced in Deuteronomy. Here is what Moses told the people about celebrating the festivals of Passover and the Feast of Weeks: *"You shall sacrifice...in the place where the Lord chooses to establish his name... and you shall rejoice before the Lord your God, you and your son and your daughter and your male and female servants and the Levite who is in your town, and the stranger and the orphan and the widow who are in your midst, in the place where the Lord your God chooses to establish his name."* (Deut. 16: 2,11.)

In the Old Testament we saw that to have God's Name is to have his presence. When the Israelites came into the Promised Land, they built the temple in Jerusalem. The people of God could not celebrate the festivals of Passover, the Feast of Weeks (our Pentecost) and other festival days just anywhere. They had to celebrate them in the place where God chose to set his name—in his presence. It is important to see that everyone got to participate. Feasting in God's presence was for all who were in the Promised Land, from the richest land owners to the poorest widows and orphans. There was no discrimination between who could rejoice in the goodness of God and who couldn't. In fact, everyone's attendance was expected. In the same way today, our Father God invites all who are found in Christ to feast in his presence. Under the new covenant established by Jesus' death, burial and resurrection, God's Name and presence are found in his Son Jesus.

God Loves the Place Where his Name Dwells

Solomon's prayer at the dedication of the temple once again shows us the relationship between God's Name and his presence: *"O Lord my God, listen to the prayer which Your servant prays before You; that Your eye may be open toward this house day and night,* **toward the place of which You have said that You would put Your name there,** *to listen to the prayer which Your servant shall pray toward this place...hear from Your dwelling place, from heaven; hear and forgive...v. 32 Also concerning the foreigner who is not from Your people Israel, when he comes from a far country for Your great name's sake...when they come and pray toward this house, then hear from heaven, from Your dwelling place, and do according to all for which the foreigner calls to You,* **in order that all the peoples of the earth may know Your name**, *and fear You as do Your people Israel, and* **that they may know that this house which I have built is called by Your name** *"* (II Chronicles 6:19-21; 32-33).

God's house is the place where he lives. That is the place called by his Name. Today, when we call on the name of Jesus, we enter the dwelling of God. How wonderful! That has both personal and corporate implications. On a personal level, we can experience the Lord as our dwelling place because he has given us his Name. On the corporate level, as we live in his presence the Lord will inevitably lead us into greater relationship with others in his body, the church. That's because we were made to be part of something greater than ourselves.

Here was God's response to Solomon's prayer: *"Now my eyes shall be open and my ears attentive to the prayer offered in this place. For now I have chosen and consecrated this house* **that my name may be there forever, and my eyes and my heart will be there perpetually***"* (II Chronicles 7:15-16).

These beautiful verses show us once again that God's dwelling place in the heavens can be accessed from earth. The connecting point is the place where God has put his name. His eyes are open to that place. His ear is attentive to that place. His heart will be there perpetually. He can hear prayer, he can answer, and he can forgive. What is that place? That place is Christ and, by extension, the body of which he is the head. The Lord tried to explain this wondrous mystery to his disciples in the following conversation with Philip found in John 14: 6: *"Jesus said to him, 'I am the way, and the truth, and the life; no one comes to the Father but through me. If you had known me, you would have known my Father also; from now on you know him, and have seen him.' Philip said to him, 'Lord, show us the Father, and it is enough for us.' Jesus said to him, 'Have I been so long with you, and yet you have not come to know me, Philip? He who has seen me has seen the Father; how can you say, "Show us the Father"? Do you not believe that I am in the Father, and the Father is in me?'"*

The Lord Came in the Father's Name

The Lord made it plain that he had come in the Father's Name. Here are his words from John 5:43: *"I have come in my Father's name, and you do not receive me; if another shall come in his own name, you will receive him."* Jesus was the representation of the Father, but the people could not see it and did not receive him.

In John 10:25, the Lord said this: *"I told you, and you do not believe; the works that I do in my Father's name, these bear witness of me. But you do not believe because you are not of my sheep. My sheep hear my voice, and I know them, and they follow me; and I give eternal life to them, and they will never perish; and no one will snatch them out of my hand. My Father, who has given them to me, is greater than all; and no one is able to snatch them out of the Father's hand. I and the Father are one."*

These verses reveal that God the Father dwelt in Christ the Son and that Jesus acted under his Father's authority and carried out his Father's will. He was a person on the earth who brought into plain view the Name, the authority and the will of the Father in the heavens. That will is for us to receive the eternal life of God. God's enemy, of course, was totally opposed to such a development. He didn't want a man on the earth acting in the Name of the Lord and showing forth the attributes of the living God. He knew that under such conditions, his power was broken. In light of that, the response to Jesus' words should not shock us. The Jews picked up rocks to stone him. The enemy did not want this Name exalted then. He does not want it exalted now.

God's Enemy Opposes this Name

Those who make up the body of Christ have been called out of darkness to make his name known. This is what Peter did in Acts 2:38 where we read, *"Then Peter said unto them, Repent, and let each of you be baptized* **in the name of Jesus Christ** *for the forgiveness of sins, and you shall receive the gift of the Holy Spirit."* We see Peter in action again in Acts 3:6: *"But Peter said, 'I do not possess silver and gold, but what I do have I give to you:* **In the name of Jesus Christ** *the Nazarene—walk'"* and in Acts 4:12 where he declared, *"And there is salvation in no one else: for* **there is no other name under heaven that has been given among men, by which we must be saved.** *"* Peter was well aware of the power of this great name.

The authorities responded to Peter the same way they did to Jesus. The Jewish leaders warned the disciples not to speak any longer in this name. *"And when they had summoned them,* **they commanded them not to speak or teach at all in the name of Jesus.** *But Peter and John answered and said to them, 'Whether it is right in the sight of God to give heed to you rather than to God, you be the judge; for we cannot stop speaking about what we have seen and heard'"* (Acts 4:18). The disciples knew that it was in the name of Jesus that their strength and testimony lay. They were totally enthralled with Jesus and could not help but speak of him to anyone who would listen. The fact that they had been made a part of his family and given his name was real. They had to spread this incredible news. When they were released, they immediately went back to proclaiming the excellencies of his name no matter the consequences. They were taken into custody again, and this time the Jewish leaders wanted to kill them. But a Pharisee named Gamaliel intervened on their behalf. Acts 5:40 records what happened: *"And they took his* [Gamaliel's] *advice: and after calling the apostles in, they flogged them and ordered them to speak no more* **in the name of Jesus**, *and then they released them."*

The disciples responded by counting it an honor to suffer for his name. *"So they went on their way from the presence of the Council, rejoicing that they had been considered worthy to* **suffer shame for his name**. *And every day, in the temple and from house to house, they kept right on teaching and preaching Jesus as the Christ"* (Acts 5:41-42). For first century believers, speaking forth the name of Jesus meant declaring to the nations that Christ was alive, that he is the one who saves us from this present evil age and that he has invited us to partake of the riches found in his name. Based on this testimony of who Christ is, the church is built and the gates of hell will not stand against it.

The Name Above All Names

In what name do we trust? Whose names are we exalting? Are we looking to ourselves for sufficiency and success, or to mentors or friends to whom we can hitch our star? Or have we found that there is a name that is above every name that we can turn to? It is a blessed day when we discover that the name of Jesus is the entry way into a whole new realm of living. As the apostle John put it in John 20:31, *"these things have been written that you may believe that Jesus is the Christ, the Son of God; and that believing* **you may have life in his name**.*"*

Matthew 28:18 gives more insight into the importance of the Lord's name: *"Jesus spoke to them, saying, 'All authority has been given to Me in heaven and on earth. Go therefore and make disciples of all the nations,* **baptizing them in the name** *of the Father and the Son and the Holy Spirit, teaching them to observe all that I commanded you; and lo, I am with you always, even to the end of the age.'"* The word "baptized" here means being placed or immersed into. Through faith in Christ we are baptized (placed) into the name of the Father, Son and Spirit. From

God's perspective that means we are immersed in all that the Father is, all that the Son is and all that the Spirit is. What a glorious location! All the attributes of that great Name are available to us. Christ becomes our residence, our strength, our place of refuge. We, in turn become the dwelling place of our Lord. Best of all, he is with us always, even until the end of the age. His presence makes all things possible.

Doing all in Jesus' name does not mean that he sends you out to do errands on his behalf while he waits for you back at home. No. You live in him and he lives in you. You exalt his Name by following his Spirit within you, giving him the credit that he deserves for the good things that happen as a result.

The Eternal Depth of the Lord's Name

In closing, be aware that there is nothing more precious or powerful to Jesus Christ than the name of the Father, Son and Spirit. Listen to his words in John 14:13: *"Whatever you ask in my name, that will I do, so that the Father may be glorified in the Son. If you ask me anything in my name, I will do it."* These are powerful words. The Lord Jesus loves to see his Father glorified. So it is important that we learn how to ask in the Lord's name. This does not mean that if we pray in Jesus' name for a new car, we will get a new BMW (though many try to make prayers like that work). No, the Lord has something far greater on his mind than new BMWs.

In John 14:1-3, Jesus told his disciples that he was going into his Father's realm in the heavens to make a place for them. Where he was, his disciples would be also. Here are his familiar words: *"Let not your heart be troubled; believe in God, believe also in me. In my Father's house are many dwelling places; if it were not so, I would have told you; for I go to prepare a place for you. If I go and prepare a place for you, I will come again and receive you to myself, that where I am, there you may be also."* While this passage is often interpreted to mean that Jesus was going to heaven to make a place for us when we die (which he did), the context of the passage does not refer to future events. It refers rather to something that would happen soon. Jesus went on to say in verses 6 and 7, *"I am the way, and the truth, and the life; no one comes to the Father but through me. If you had known me, you would have known my Father also; from now on you know him, and have seen him."* These verses show that the access that Jesus was opening to the Father was to begin for his disciples then, not when they died or at the end of the ages. In verse 12, he added, *"Truly, truly, I say to you, he who believes in me, the works that I do, he will do also; and greater works than these he will do; because I go to the Father."* Jesus was referring to deeds that his disciples would do in his name after he had physically departed.

Jesus is issuing an invitation to explore the depths of who God is and to join in with all he wants to do. Because we have been placed into Christ, we can discover things in heavenly realms that the Father wants done, and we can ask the Lord to do them. According to Jesus' promise, he will make such things happen. These words are an encouragement for us to find our place in Christ, where he speaks, communicating the Father's will to us.

There is a common thread between these verses and Jesus' words to Peter in Matthew 16:17, *"Jesus said to him, 'Blessed are you, Simon Barjona, because flesh and blood did not reveal this to you, but My Father who is in heaven. I also say to you that you are Peter, and upon this rock I will build My church; and the gates of Hades shall not overpower it; I will give you the keys of the kingdom of heaven; and whatever you bind on earth shall be bound in heaven, and whatever you loose on earth shall be loosed in heaven.'"* What glorifies the Father and the Son is the will of God carried out on the earth by Jesus Christ through his church. Now that's glorious; even more glorious than a new BMW.

These are important matters. How can such deep truths be turned into practical reality in our lives? Jesus told his disciples, *"These things I have spoken to you while abiding with you. But the Helper, the Holy Spirit,* **whom the Father will send in my name***, he will teach you all things, and bring to your remembrance all that I said to you. Peace I leave with you; my peace I give to you; not as the world gives do I give to you. Do not let your heart be troubled, nor let it be fearful. You heard that I said to you, 'I go away, and I will come to you'"* (John 14:25-28). The Lord wants us to be at peace. You do not have to worry about how the Lord will work this out in your life. Jesus comes to you as Spirit to make the riches of his great name available to you. As you turn to him, he will teach you how to live in his presence. He will make known to you the wonder of who he is. He is the author and perfecter of your faith.

In his prayer to his Father before going to the cross, Jesus prayed, "**I have manifested your name** *to the men whom you gave me out of the world; they were yours and you gave them to me, and they have kept your word...I am no longer in the world; and yet they themselves are in the world, and I come to you.* **Holy Father, keep them in your name, the name which you have given me**, *that they may be one even as We are...O righteous Father, although the world has not known you, yet I have known you; and these have known that you sent me;* **and I have made your name known to them, and will make it known, so that the love with which you loved me may be in them, and I in them.**" (John 17:6, 11, 25-26)

These deep words will take an eternity to fully understand. Here we learn that to manifest the Father's name means to reveal his character, to show what he is really like. He asked his Father that we would be kept in his name—held tight in his loving presence. This is the New Testament way of expressing the verse in Proverbs quoted earlier, *"The name of the Lord is a strong tower, I will run into it and be safe."* Our minds can only begin to grasp how vast and strong that tower really is. But Jesus knows. He made it clear that he had only started to reveal to his followers the wonders found in his Father's glorious presence. He will continue to show forth those wonders through endless ages. These are more than words on a page or truths to be learned. This is our inheritance and our destiny.

If it is not your practice to daily encounter the Lord by calling on his name, why not start today? You can whisper his name or you can shout it. You can groan it, sigh it, sing it or speak it. You can call it out while driving in your car, sitting at your desk, standing at the stove, or finishing this sentence. But by all means, join the company of believers who from the first century on have been taking advantage of being on a first name basis with the King of Kings and Lord of Lords. They have called on him in times of trouble and in times of rejoicing. They have called on him at work and at play, at school and in battle. They have called on him alone and in the company of others.

The results of spending time with the Lord, allowing him to saturate you from within with his being and life, are oneness and love. Can you imagine being loved by God the way that he loves Jesus Christ? You are. Can you imagine experiencing the same degree of unity with your brothers and sisters that the Father shares with the Son? That is God's goal for us. These are wonderful truths to consider.

God's amazing plan for you and me begins with the Lord's Name. When you feel a longing to be in the Lord's presence, respond by calling on him. He has placed that longing in your heart. The Lord is committed to making the greatness of God known to you.

Join in the quest to recapture the richness found in the Lord's name. You can start by taking an honest look at your uses of his name, eliminating the superficial or mechanical ones. There are deeper waters waiting in your experience with him. As the Psalmist wrote so long ago, *"The Lord is near to all who* **call** *upon him, to all who call upon him in truth"* (Psalm 145:18). He is near to you now. Say his name. Let his name wash over you. Let his name warm your heart and fill you with the joy and closeness found in his presence. He will hear your call.

The Cross

"But may it never be that I should boast, except in the cross of our Lord Jesus Christ" Gal. 6:14

Cross symbols are common today in many parts of the world. Cross jewelry is popular among Christians who know its meaning. The movie *The Passion of the Christ* revealed to millions the excruciating brutality that Christ suffered in going to the cross. Those who wear a cross with that knowledge honor the sacrifice given there. But cross symbols are also popular among artists, athletes, movie stars and others and, for some, they are no more than fashion statements or good luck charms.

What happened at the cross is the pivotal event of human history. Through the cross God was fully unleashed to carry out his eternal plan. Your destiny and mine will be decided by our acceptance of what God accomplished there through Jesus Christ. Therefore we must take a careful look at what the cross meant for God and what it means for us. Jesus' death on the cross and his subsequent resurrection set him apart from every other person, prophet or religious leader. While every religion accepts Jesus in some form or other, only Christianity exalts **Christ and him crucified.** Only a crucified Jesus will take care of the problem of sin that impacts the human race. As the writer of Hebrews put it, *"And according to the Law...all things are cleansed with blood, and without shedding of blood there is no forgiveness"* (Hebrews 9:22).

For many Christians, the mention of the cross as it relates to our lives can be intimidating. We are ever thankful for the cross, because we know that Christ's death there meant our salvation. But when we encounter verses like those in Mark 8:34-35 where Jesus says, *"If anyone wishes to come after me, he must deny himself, and take up his cross and follow me,"* we get nervous. We are not sure what the implications are of having the cross applied to our lives. Those implications can be scary. Such verses may leave us feeling resigned to a life of denying much of what we deem enjoyable. Perhaps the image of priests and nuns living in cloistered silence and celibacy has added to such fears. We want to follow Christ, but we don't feel called to such a lifestyle. God's enemy feeds into our insecurity by presenting to us the image of a life lived in the doldrums, where we are at the mercy of a strict God waiting to punish us whenever we get out of line. Such thoughts have nothing to do with Christ's real accomplishment at the cross. If such thinking bogs you down, this is the time to recapture the glorious truth regarding the cross of Christ and its impact on your life.

What propelled God to send his Son to the cross? What was the driving energy that caused God to carry out such a painful plan? You know the answer. It was his love. God so loved the world that he gave his only begotten Son. Love was behind the activity of the cross in the life of Christ. Likewise, love is behind the daily crosses that God sends us to bear. We are used to seeing crosses placed in church buildings and on flags or used as emblems. Those don't impact us much. But we must be secure in the love of God to respond with openness when the Lord asks us to embrace the practical work of the cross in our personal lives.

Jesus was secure in his Father's love. He knew the glory that was waiting for him (and you) on the other side of that cross. That's why he could follow his Father wherever the Father led him, even to his death. Because of that death the love of God and the eternal provision he made for believers in Christ —making them part of his own family—is now yours to experience through faith in him.

Take Up Your Cross and Follow Me

The Lord talked about the cross with his disciples before the crucifixion. He wanted them to know in advance that while the cross would be the instrument of his death, its work would also yield benefits for those who followed him. *"And he began to teach them that the Son of Man must suffer many things and be rejected by the elders and the chief priests and the scribes, and be killed, and after three days rise again. And he was stating the matter plainly. And Peter took him aside and began to rebuke him. But turning around and seeing his disciples, he rebuked Peter and said, 'Get behind me, Satan; for you are not setting your mind on God's interests, but man's.' And he summoned the crowd with his disciples, and said to them, 'If anyone wishes to come after me, he must deny himself, and take up his cross and follow me. For whoever wishes to save his life will lose it, but whoever loses his life for my sake and the gospel's will save it. For what does it profit a man to gain the whole world, and forfeit his soul?'"* (Mark 8:31-36).

At this point in his ministry, Jesus taught openly that he would have to suffer many things, including rejection and death. Notice that he described himself as the Son of Man. This suffering was not his because he was the Son of God. No, this suffering came to him because he had taken the form of a man. He undertook this suffering on our behalf. Peter's reaction was startling. He took Jesus aside and began to rebuke him. This tells us something about the approachableness and humility of the Lord Jesus. The creator of the universe, the son of God, the miracle worker, was so humble that Peter, a fisherman, felt the freedom to pull him aside and rebuke him. Evidently Jesus did not "lord it over" his followers or strike fear into their hearts. Thank God, he didn't then and he doesn't now.

We could look down on Peter. We could criticize him for his stupidity. But if we had been in his position, you or I might have done the same thing. We are not less fallen or less protective of ourselves than he was at that moment. Peter didn't like where Jesus was going with all this talk of suffering and death, especially death by crucifixion. This was the most shameful of deaths, reserved for the worst criminals. From Peter's view things were going fine. Jesus was getting famous. Lots of people were following him. People were getting fed, even healed. And, perhaps best of all, Peter was in Jesus' inner circle. Why mess it up by talking about rejection and death?

It's reasonable to think that Peter was looking down the road at what might happen to Jesus' followers if Jesus were killed. Not only would Peter's hopes of future glory be dashed, but he might be in actual danger. Obviously the part about being raised up in three days hadn't sunk in very far. But we can hardly blame Peter for that. At that point in time the number of people that he knew who had died and been resurrected amounted to zero.

But Jesus was not humored by Peter's rebuke. Nor did he make any attempt to sugar-coat his response: *"Get behind Me, Satan; for you are not setting your mind on God's interests, but man's."* What are man's interests? In this case, man's interests were maintaining the status quo—not rocking the boat—and self preservation. Man's interests did not include the admission that a sacrificial death was needed to cover sin. Man's interests included the protection of the soul and staying away from any denial of the self. All of these things actually reflected Satan's interests as well, allowing him to retain his control over a sinful humanity.

God is Interested in Us

But God's interests were far different. God was interested in redeeming the sinful human race. He was interested in making his creation whole. God was interested in fellowship, in being in union with his people, in sharing his glory with them. He wanted to crush his enemy and see his son Jesus magnified. God loved his creation and knew that to go on with the status quo would result in his precious creation perishing, lost in sin. As John 3:16 reminds us, *"For God so loved the world that he gave his only begotten son that whoever believes in him should not perish but have eternal life."* If Jesus had harkened to Peter's rebuke, the result would have been Peter's perishing. Peter didn't know that. He didn't know that the status quo was that the enemy had taken control of mankind. He didn't know that the end of all things for man was eternal death.

But God the Father knew it. His interests centered on saving mankind from that fate. His interest wasn't in punishment. His interest was in redemption, on making things whole. But God's enemy, Satan, had infiltrated man's thinking. The enemy had no desire to see his captives released. Jesus knew where Peter's message was coming from and directly addressed the source. With his words, *"Get behind me, Satan,"* Jesus let his enemy know that nothing could stop him from ending Satan's tyrannical reign over mankind.

Satan also knew that Jesus' obedience to the Father was his greatest obstacle in overcoming the power that Jesus had over him. If Jesus would abandon the path of obedience that he was on, Satan would once again triumph over man as he had in the Garden of Eden. But Jesus was not swayed. He let his followers know that not only was his path leading him to the cross, but it would lead them there as well. There the power of Satan would be crushed.

When Jesus invited his followers to follow him, he was fully aware that the journey would not end at the cross. On the other side of the cross Jesus was going back to his Father, to be seated in heavenly places. As Paul wrote, *"These are in accordance with the working of the strength of God's might, which he brought about in Christ, when he raised him from the dead and seated him at his right hand in the heavenly places"* (Ephesians 1:19-20). Jesus was fully confident of that when he said, *"If anyone wants to come after me, let him take up his cross and follow me."* He sat down at the right hand of God. That's where he was going, and we have been invited to go there with him. The road to that heavenly seat goes through the cross.

Jesus made it clear that not only was forgiveness of sin a necessity to follow him, but the receiving of a new life, as well. That's why he said in Mark 8, *"whoever wishes to save his life shall lose it, but whoever loses his life for my sake and the gospel's will save it."* The literal word for "lose" in that passage is "destroy." Jesus knew that he was the only solution for the power of death that had infected man. That's why he said, *"I am the way, the truth and the life, no one comes to the Father but through me."* If we are not in Christ, we are in the realm of his enemy, Satan. The enemy's purpose for man is destruction. Following Jesus, on the other hand, leads to life eternal.

The Benefits Multiply

It's significant that Jesus said, *"For my sake and the gospel's."* We are not just taking up our cross for Jesus' sake. There is another reason for us to deny ourselves and follow Christ. It is not just for him, nor is it just for us personally. The Lord is building a body, a kingdom, a city, and a bride. This is the full gospel. When we take up our cross and follow Jesus, the whole building benefits. When we lay down our egos, our pride, our selfishness, and our destructive behaviors to choose Christ, the body of Christ is strengthened.

At the cross, our sinful natures were dealt with. The cross becomes our ally in bringing us into the heavenlies, where Jesus is seated. There grace and mercy are ours in abundance. Peter did not initially understand why Jesus needed to die on his behalf. But as he later wrote to believers everywhere, *"he himself bore our sins in his body on the cross, so that we might die to sin and live to righteousness; for by his wounds you were healed"* (1 Peter 2:24). Later in that same letter he wrote, *"Therefore, since Christ has suffered in the flesh, arm yourselves also with the same purpose, because he who has suffered in the flesh has ceased from sin, so as to live the rest of the time in the flesh no longer for the lusts of men, but for the will of God"* (I Peter 4:1-2).

That will, as revealed in John 3:16, is that we would not perish but have eternal life. That life would be transmitted to us by Christ the life giving Spirit. As Peter put it, *"For Christ also died for sins once for all, the just for the unjust, so that he might bring us to God, having been put to death in the flesh, but made alive in the spirit"* (1 Peter 3:18). At the cross our Lord put death to death and was released as the Spirit to make life and immortality available to us.

The Cross and the Building

Luke 14 tells the story of Jesus being followed by huge multitudes. He has healed, turned water into wine, mass-produced food, driven out demons and spoken with authority. If he were interested in establishing an earthly kingdom, this would be the time to rally the forces. But instead Jesus chose to drive home the message of the cross.

As the crowds pressed in on him, Jesus yelled out, *"If anyone comes to me, and does not hate his own father and mother and wife and children and brothers and sisters, yes, and even his own life, he cannot be my disciple. Whoever does not carry his own cross and come after me cannot be my disciple."*

Ouch.

Hate my father, hate my mother, carry a cross? Those were hard words to swallow. What about more free food? What about getting rid of the oppressive Roman government? But let's not overlook Jesus' opening words... *"if anyone comes to me."* From God's perspective this is what it's all about: coming to Jesus. Do you want to come to him? Do you want to hang out with him? This is the central question regarding the Lord Jesus. Being with him makes whatever follows worthwhile. As Jesus put it before going to that cross, *"Father, I desire that they also, whom you have given me, be with me where I am, so that they may see my glory which you have given me, for you loved me before the foundation of the world"* (John 17:24). The purpose of the cross is getting us to where Jesus is so that we can experience life with him. Don't let this truth get lost in his challenging words.

Considering what Jesus said, it is fair to consider if there is any indication that Jesus despised his mother. The evidence shows otherwise. In fact, as he hung dying on the cross, Jesus made sure his mother would be cared for. And there is certainly no New Testament injunction that encourages husbands to hate their wives. Just the opposite is true. Paul exhorted the Ephesian believers to love their wives, *as Christ loved the church*, and gave himself up for it. So obviously, Jesus was saying something deeper here than his literal words imply. Some say that Jesus was trying to draw a comparison for us. The idea is that our love for Jesus is to be so great that, in contrast, our love for those closest to us seems like hate. But if we are honest with ourselves we have to say that even that is not the case. Most of us cannot honestly say that we love Jesus so much that our feelings for our parents, spouses and children seem like hate.

So what's the point? It's my conclusion that what Jesus was asking here is impossible. Under the conditions Jesus sets forth, it is impossible for us to be his disciples. While that may seem shocking, it shouldn't be. As Paul wrote many years later to the Corinthians, *"by his doing you are in Christ Jesus, who became to us wisdom from God, and righteousness and sanctification, and redemption, so that, just as it is written, 'LET HIM WHO BOASTS, BOAST IN THE LORD'"* (1 Corinthians 1:30-31). Jesus was letting that vast crowd know that something more than just their good intentions or a passing interest in the things of God were necessary to follow him; there would be a cost involved. They could not do it on their own. They would need the power of a greater life.

Jesus spelled out the cost in his following words: *"For which one of you when he wants to build a tower does not first sit down and calculate the costs to see if he has enough to complete it? Otherwise when he has laid a foundation and is not able to finish, all who observe him begin to ridicule him saying, This man began to build and was not able to finish."* (Luke 14:28-30). When God started to build his kingdom on earth, Jesus Christ was the cornerstone of that building. When Jesus was in Jerusalem, he walked past the temple with his disciples. The disciples were amazed by its beautiful stones and buildings. Jesus made the preposterous statement that if the temple were destroyed, in three days he would raise it up. These words revealed that he was on a mission to build the real house of God.

Jesus' words about the temple evidently were spread all over town. Surely there was some snickering going on as the rumor spread. Perhaps even his own disciples thought he had gone too far this time. Was Jesus going to lead an insurrection that involved tearing down the precious temple? How could anyone build such a glorious building in three days? Little did his detractors know how great that building would become. When Jesus stood trial before the Jewish authorities, these words were thrown back in his face. Accusers stood before him and testified, *"This man stated, 'I am able to destroy the temple of God and to rebuild it in three days'"* (Matthew 26:61). Later on, when Jesus hung on the cross, his words were once again used to taunt and humiliate him. *"Those passing by were hurling abuse at him, wagging their heads and saying, 'You who are going to destroy the temple and rebuild it in three days, save yourself! If you are the Son of God, come down from the cross.' In the same way the chief priests also, along with the scribes and elders, were mocking him and saying, he saved others; he cannot save himself"* (Matthew 27:39-42).

In Luke 14 Jesus warned those who followed him that the day would come when those who built for his kingdom would be accused of not having counted the cost; that they would be ridiculed for not being able to finish what they had started. His very words came true in his own life. As Jesus hung on the cross, to the world it certainly seemed as if he did not finish what he had come to start. After all, there he hung dying, with no one to save him. But Jesus had counted the cost. He knew that it would cost him everything to bring his Father's plan to successful completion. He had utter faith that his Father would raise him up again by the power of an indestructible life. Jesus Christ needed the help of the eternal life of his Father to complete this building. As Peter declared at Pentecost, *"But God raised him up again, putting an end to the agony of death, since it was impossible for him to be held in its power."* (Acts 2:24)

Just as Jesus Christ needed the life of his Father to carry out his part of the building, you and I need the same. If we follow Jesus, we can be sure that days will come when we feel we cannot finish what we've started, that being a Christian requires more than we can give. At such times even our thoughts will testify against us, accusing us of not having what it takes to live the Christian life at the level Jesus seemingly demands. But if we did have what it takes to live the Christian life, we wouldn't have needed the cross. I can count the cost of being a believer all day long, but in the end there is only one way I can do it. That is through the life of the Lord Jesus Christ living in me, empowering me with his life. That is the message of the cross. On our own, we do not have what it takes to live as Christians. Simply put, we need Jesus. In moments of doubt God is closer than we can know, waiting to encourage us in our desperation that he is the One who has called us and he is the One who perfects the work that he has begun in us. We need the power of a resurrected Christ. Thank God, it was made available to us through the cross.

The Cross Makes Us Salty

Jesus went on to let the crowd know what his expectations were. He said, *"Or what king, when he sets out to meet another king in battle, will not first sit down and take counsel whether he is strong enough with ten thousand men to encounter the one coming against him with twenty thousand? Or else, while the other is still far away, he sends a delegation and asks for terms of peace. So therefore, none of you can be my disciple who does not give up all his own possessions. Therefore, salt is good; but if even salt has become tasteless, with what will it be seasoned? It is useless either for the soil or for the manure pile; it is thrown out. He who has ears to hear, let him hear"* (Luke 14:31-35).

In this passage the Lord groups going out to war, giving up our possessions and the value of salt in a most provocative way. These illustrations followed the Lord's admonition that those wanting to be his disciples had to pick up their cross and follow him.

Consider the illustration of the kings. A king with ten thousand men is about to encounter a king with twenty thousand men who is steadily moving into his territory. Those are not good odds for the first king. The implication is that if he is smart, he will send out a delegation to ask for terms of peace and to find out what it will cost him to enjoy that peace.

There's much that we can take from this illustration. The king with the greater strength is Jesus. He is the king of glory who has come to conquer us with his love. The lesser king is us. We're the ones Jesus wants to rule over. To our eternal gain, he is stronger, and he will win this battle. We see him coming and if we're smart, we're thinking, "Whoa, I'd better ask for peace. Lord, what is it going to take to have peace with you?" Jesus' response is all-consuming.

"I want everything you have!"

Jesus' terms of peace are that he wants everything! No matter how much or how little you may think you have, he wants it all! It was as if Jesus put up a sign that said, "Follow me at your own risk." This is the gospel. One can only imagine the thoughts that must have swept through that crowd. Those masses following Jesus to see what they might get next finally got to see the price tag. He was demanding everything from them.

Jesus wants everything we've got. That doesn't mean he wants us to be poor. No, that would be too easy. He wants us to reach our highest potential and then turn it all over to him, including our very lives. He wants us to come to him and say, "Okay, Lord, you can have it all! Use it any way you see fit." That's a challenge worth responding to. Are we talking here about possessions? Yes. Are we talking about our careers? Yes. Are we talking about our families? Yes. He wants it all.

That doesn't mean that the Lord's highest purpose is for you and me to sell everything and go overseas to be missionaries. Many people have gotten the message that to follow Christ at the most committed level means they will become some type of minister or missionary, or that God places a higher value on that which is called "Christian service." While God does call some to such endeavors, that message is incorrect. God does not place a higher value on one kind of vocation over another. No, God wants you to live for him right where you are, with the talents and interests he's given you, in the midst of a society that has little idea of what it means to be truly free.

My wife, Christie, and I have given up everything we own several times. We once lived in a situation where for several years we pooled all our possessions with other believers. We've lived overseas, and we've moved across the United States three times. We know what it's like to pinch pennies. But we have also lived in some of the world's most beautiful locations. Our four children all went to excellent universities. We own a nice home and have decent cars. But the Lord might ask us to leave those possessions behind and start somewhere new tomorrow. We would have a choice to make. Do we want to follow him into new adventures of faith, or do we want to camp where we are?

He could ask for it. He's done it before, he might do it again. But following Jesus is not about having things or not having things. No, the issue with Jesus is where our hearts are. Do we want to make peace with him? He knows that the greatest peace comes when all that we have is turned over to him.

Following the parable about the kings, Jesus moved on to talk about salt. *"Therefore salt is good."* Where was Jesus going now? In the Lord's mind, what is good is living life in fellowship with him where he is in charge of all we possess. As you follow this Christ you become very salty! You add pungency to this planet. People who aren't afraid to follow Jesus as he works in their families, in their workplaces, in their social circles, in their church fellowships and in the planet at large add true flavor to this world.

But if the salt loses its flavor, it is good for nothing! It's not good for seasoning, it's not good for the soil, it's not even good for manure. Jesus called us the salt of the world. We keep that saltiness by following him. He is free from the bonds of this world. He broke through death at the cross and freed us from its grip. Jesus calls to us and encourages us not to be afraid. Let him have what you've got. He'll take care of it. He may add to it. He may enrich it. He may have a bigger idea for your life than you could have thought possible. The opposite of saltiness is blandness. The Lord has better things in mind for you.

To become the salt that God intends us to be, we need the work of the cross in our lives. Our natural inclination is toward security and safety. We don't want to face the possibility of rejection. We don't want to risk looking stupid. On top of that, the enemy seeks to lull us into complacency with earthly distractions. Many opt for a Jesus who saves them from their sins but isn't allowed to be too active in their lives. From Jesus' point of view, that kind of Christian living isn't worth much. The more we live in fellowship with him, the more flavorful our lives become. How do we get there from here? We follow Jesus. We surrender our lives to the Jesus who went to the cross and yet lives again. Following the crucified Christ will cost you everything. But you will get more in return than you could ever imagine.

The Cross Unleashes Jesus

Believers know that Jesus died on the cross for their sins, and that it's important to follow him; but many aren't sure how the work of the cross practically impacts their lives. Paul explained this in several New Testament passages. In I Corinthians 1:17-19 Paul writes, *"Christ did not send me to baptize, but to preach the gospel, not in cleverness of speech, that the cross of Christ should not be made void. For the word of the cross is to those who are perishing foolishness, but to us who are being saved it is the power of God."*

The Corinthians were evidently dividing themselves according to various workers who had come to Corinth. To counter that, Paul said his primary mission was preaching the gospel in such a way that the message of the cross wouldn't lose its teeth. He reminded them that it appeared stupid to talk to people about the cross. The Lord Jesus encountered that with Peter when Peter pulled him aside and told him not to go to the cross. But Paul had come to understand that all are perishing due to sin, and that outside of the cross there is no way to deal with that sin. He admitted this sounded foolish to those who would rather play lofty mind games about the goodness of man, or the origin of the universe. But they were perishing! So Paul thundered out that the message of the cross was the power of God for those who were being saved.

The cross turns loose the power of God because the cross unleashed Jesus Christ to become the life-giving Spirit. Paul put it this way: *"The first Adam became a living soul, the last Adam a life giving spirit."* Jesus Christ died on the cross as the Son of Man. He was resurrected by the eternal Spirit and, as Paul put it in Romans 1:4, *"he was declared the Son of God with power by the resurrection from the dead, according to the Spirit of holiness, Jesus Christ our Lord."* After his resurrection Jesus ascended into heavenly realms and was glorified. Then he re-entered the physical world with the ability to breathe his Spirit into those who would receive him. The cross unleashes the power of God into your life when you accept Christ by faith. When we preach Christ crucified, we also preach Christ resurrected, the power of God and the wisdom of God. As the life-giving Spirit, he wants to set us free from death; free from pride; free from sin; free from loneliness and fear; free to live a fruitful life.

No More Body Casts

When my wife, Christie, was a teen-ager, she had a curved spine, known as scoliosis. To solve that problem, doctors put her in a body cast. The cast extended from her neck to her waist and she wore it for a year. Somehow the mere presence of that cast was supposed to change the direction of her spine. (Sadly, it did not). It was not very comfortable or attractive, but she wore it, having been promised that it might do some good.

This may be uncomfortably close to the way many view the work of the cross. When it comes to applying the cross to their lives, many think God wants to put them in a body cast. They fear he is going to saddle them with one list of things they have to do and another list of things they can't do. Or he is going to find ways to make them suffer so that they can be better people in the end. Because they think it's for their own good, the really devout say, "Okay God, bring on the cross, bring on the body cast." The rest run for cover.

If you can relate to that mindset, take heart. That is not how God works the benefits of the cross into your life. The fact is that without Christ people are already in a body cast and don't know what to do about it. They want to soar, but they can't. They have the sense that they were made for something eternal, but they don't know how to fulfill that longing. They are bound up with sin, with guilt, with a fear of rejection, with shame, and with an impending fear that inevitably death waits out there for them. Though they may find ways to live with and cover over their inadequacies, a yearning to be free remains in their hearts. The fact is that they are in body casts. They were created for higher things, but they have been bound by an enemy who managed to alienate them from the God who made them.

If you've had such a mindset, Jesus Christ wants to cut you out of your body cast and set you free through his death on the cross. The cross released Jesus Christ to enter the lives of his followers and set them free from all that binds them. As Paul wrote to the Romans, *"Therefore there is now no condemnation for those who are in Christ Jesus. For the law of the Spirit of life in Christ Jesus has set you free from the law of sin and of death"* (Romans 8:1-2). Through his death on the cross, the Lord Jesus freed us from sin and death; now the work of the cross in our lives is to come in and to cut away what remains of the body cast. *"It was for freedom that Christ set us free"* (Galatians 5:1).

Sometimes the process of setting us free hurts. The Lord faces obstacles in transforming us into his image. Our pride stands in the way. Our flesh stands in the way. Our selfishness stands in the way. Our old habits stand in the way. Sometimes the Lord asks us to lay down what we want for his sake or for the sake of his building. That can hurt; a part of us screams, "But, it's not fair. I deserve better." On the other side of that death, however, we find new liberty and increased peace as we become less self-conscious and more conscious of the goodness and wisdom of God. That's why Paul said to the Romans, *The mind set on the flesh is death, but the mind set on the Spirit is life and peace"* (Romans 8:6).

The cross turned Jesus Christ loose so that you could receive him. He, in turn, imparts his life to you. Our part in that includes saying, "Yes, Lord, go ahead. Turn loose the power of the cross in me." At times it will hurt. Death is operating in you. But the operation ends in life. Paul made this clear to the Corinthians when he wrote, *"For we who live are constantly being delivered over to death for Jesus' sake, so that the life of Jesus also may be manifested in our mortal flesh. So death works in us, but life in you"* (II Corinthians 4: 11-12). The phrase "for Jesus' sake" is actually referring to the deadening power of Jesus that he exerts in us in order to produce new life. We are delivered over to death by Jesus just as a patient is turned over to a skilled surgeon to cut away cancerous growths that were keeping life from flourishing. Do you want the life of Jesus made manifest in your mortal flesh? Anyone who has tasted his sweet life knows that this is a result worth the cost of the surgery.

The message of the cross is ultimately one of simplicity. It's not complicated. Receive by faith the reality that Jesus' death was sufficient to cover your sins. Turn over to him the authority to set you free. The realization will follow that his love for you is great and that he does that which is in your eternal best interests. As you submit to his loving work of molding you into his image, he begins the process of setting you free.

Freed from Outward Show

So what does true freedom look like? And how should we behave while God is working on us? Many believe that certain behaviors automatically go along with being "Christian" and that we must perform them, even though internally we feel our love for the Lord is inadequate and our lives are still in disarray. Paul addressed this problem when he wrote to the Galatians, *"Those who desire to make a good showing in the flesh try to compel you to be circumcised, simply so that they will not be persecuted for the cross of Christ...but may it never be that I would boast, except in the cross of our Lord Jesus Christ, through which the world has been crucified to me, and I to the world"* (Galatians 6:12-14). The believers in Galatia were being told that while Christ was good, there were certain outward rites that they also needed to observe (i.e., circumcision, observation of certain special days, etc.) if they wanted to please God.

Paul fought against this false teaching by explaining to them that at the cross of Christ they were set free from being on a performance basis with God and others. The cross proclaims that none will ever be good enough to satisfy God with outward performance. It took the death of Christ and his resurrection presence in us to make us acceptable to God. Paul knew only too well that he had been released from all the expectations that the Law, his religion and his culture had laid on him regarding what it meant to be truly acceptable before God. He was a free man, and he wasn't going back to old ways of living. He was determined to lead as many others into freedom as possible. That world of blindness and captivity had been separated from him by the death and resurrection of his wondrous Lord. Its power to keep him in darkness was broken. As he wrote to the Colossians, *"See to it that no one takes you captive through philosophy and empty deception, according to the tradition of men, according to the elementary principles of the world, rather than according to Christ"* (Colossians 2:8). Paul had had enough of the hollow pride that comes from looking good on the outside. He would only boast in the wonderful work of Christ at the cross that had freed him from having to make an outward show and whose effective work in him actually did produce the fruit of peaceful living. The day of Christ's death on the cross marked our true independence day. We should view it as such.

How to View the Cross

Let's take a look at two amazing perspectives on the cross. We'll start with Paul. Here is what he wrote to the Philippians: *"I count all things to be loss in view of the surpassing value of knowing Christ Jesus my Lord, for whom I have suffered the loss of all things, and count them but rubbish so that I may gain Christ...that I may know him and the power of his resurrection and the fellowship of his sufferings, being conformed to his death; in order that I may attain to the resurrection from the dead"* (Philippians 3:8, 10-11).

These are stirring and challenging words. In this section of Galatians, Paul listed all the things that he could have boasted in. While there were many, he counted them all worthless in comparison to what he found in his pursuit of the Lord Jesus. He suffered much but counted that suffering as light when compared to the glory that waited ahead. He wrote to the Corinthians, *"For momentary, light affliction is producing for us an eternal weight of glory far beyond all comparison"* (II Corinthians 4:17). Without hesitation he invited all who would read his words to follow him in surrendering his life to Christ.

He did that because he was in love. Consider his words, *"For the love of Christ controls us, having concluded this, that one died for all, therefore all died; and he died for all, so that they who live might no longer live for themselves, but for him who died and rose again on their behalf"* (II Corinthians 5:14-15). Paul was in love with the Lord Jesus. He had come to understand how much the Lord loved him, even to the point of surrendering his life for Paul. That love had been poured into Paul's heart through the Spirit. Now that same love that motivated God the Father to send his Son Jesus to the cross was working in Paul. Paul wanted all those with whom he came in contact to be freed by the Lord Jesus as he had been. He knew the road to freedom ran through the cross.

But many in Paul's world were opposed to God's people being set free. They derided the message of the cross and the promise of life that lay beyond it. They were effectively closing the door to the riches that Jesus Christ died to make available to those who would receive him. Their impact so distressed Paul that it moved him to tears. He went on to write, *"For many walk, of whom I often told you and now tell you even weeping, that they are enemies of the cross of Christ whose end is destruction…who set their minds on earthly things. For our citizenship is in heaven, from which also we eagerly wait for a Savior, the Lord Jesus Christ"* (Philippians 3:18-20). The enemies of the cross would rather people be destroyed than experience the wondrous gift of life made available in Christ. At one time Paul was among them. But he had tasted the air of heaven, and a whole new world had opened up to him. Now his heart of love for the Lord and his people motivated Paul to declare the wonders of his crucified Christ and the freedom found at the cross. He wept that so many would want to close the way to the path of life, and he encouraged those who loved the Lord to hold fast to him. May the Lord fill our understanding with such a perspective and our hearts with such a love.

Who for the Joy…

Our final look at the cross centers on the one who bore its terrible pain for us, the Lord Jesus. Most believers are quite familiar with the Lord's actions on the night he was crucified. He arranged for one final meal with his closest friends before he headed for Gethsemane where he was betrayed. At that meal the Lord took bread, broke it into pieces and offered it to his followers. He then took a cup of wine and offered that to them as well. Here's how Matthew described the scene: *"Now as they were eating, Jesus took bread and praising God, gave thanks … and when he had broken it, he gave it to the disciples and said, Take, eat; this is my body. And he took a cup, and when he had given thanks, he gave it to them, saying, Drink of it, all of you; For this is My blood of the new covenant, which is being poured out for many for the forgiveness of sins"* (Matthew 26: 26-28 Amplified Bible).

Jesus knew that the purpose for which he came to this planet was at hand. He knew that an excruciating and humiliating death was only hours away. He knew that the sin and shame of a fallen humanity was about to be laid on his shoulders. Still, as he picked up the bread that represented his own body, he did something truly amazing. He praised and thanked his Father. How could he do that, knowing what lay ahead? He could be thankful that his own body would be broken for only one reason: He knew it would free him up to be received by you! *"This is my body, it's for you,"* is how the Lord explained those events to Paul in I Corinthians 11: 24. Jesus did the same thing with the cup that represented his blood. In that blood a new covenant would be born, one that is based on his righteousness made available to us. If you have received him, you have experienced the freedom found in having your slate with God wiped clean.

But Jesus wasn't done showing us how to approach the cross. *"And singing a hymn, they went out to the Mount of Olives"* (Matthew 26:30, Concordant Literal New Testament). Where did Christians learn to sing in the face of adversity? Such activity was born in that circle of friends by Jesus himself as he faced the greatest challenge in all of time and eternity. Heading towards the most excruciating death known to man, the sinless Lord gathered his band of soon-to-be brothers around him and showed them how to face trials.

He began to sing.

The Lord, who had already praised and thanked his Father for what was about to be unleashed through his death and resurrection, knew what they did not: that his God was about to unloose the cords of death that had bound mankind almost since the day of creation. He knew that because of what he was about to endure the whole family of God would come to experience the love, oneness and fellowship with his Father that he experienced. He knew that, energized by his Spirit, they would go out in his Name and set captive ones free all over the earth. As he considered the freedom and life that was soon to be made available to those with him in that room—and one day to you—that brought him joy. He must have dreaded what lay immediately before him. His soul screamed within him to try and escape the coming wrath. We know that from his words in the garden of Gethsemane, *"Father, if it be possible, let this cup pass from me,"* and from the blood that he sweated as he prayed there. Nonetheless, as he considered it all, the joy of what was set before him rose to the surface, and Jesus began to sing.

What song could have been on his lips? Maybe it was a declaration of God's closeness, as a song taken from Psalm 32 describes: *"You are my hiding place, you always fill my heart with songs of deliverance, whenever I am afraid, I will trust in you."* Perhaps it was a prayer of dependence, as in Psalm 25: *"Unto you, O Lord, do I lift up my soul; oh my God, I trust in you, let me not be ashamed, let not my enemies triumph over me."* It could have been a song declaring the reality of what was about to take place based on Psalm 125: *"When the LORD brought back the captive ones of Zion, We were like those who dream. Then our mouth was filled with laughter and our tongue with joyful shouting; then they said among the nations, The LORD has done great things for them. The LORD has done great things for us; we are glad. Restore our captivity, O LORD, as the streams in the South. Those who sow in tears shall reap with joyful shouting. He, who goes to and fro weeping, carrying his bag of seed, shall indeed come again with a shout of joy, bringing his sheaves with him."*

The Lord led his disciples to the place of his betrayal singing. What a Savior! He could go to the cross in this way because he knew a loving Father was waiting for him with open arms on the other side. In God's wondrous plan, we were included in that death. As Paul put it so beautifully, *"Do you not know that all of us who have been baptized into Christ Jesus have been baptized into his death? Therefore we have been buried with him through baptism into death, in order that as Christ was raised from the dead through the glory of the Father, so we too might walk in newness of life"* (Romans 6:3-4). Now that loving Father waits for us, as well. Newness of life in his presence awaits all who are willing to pick up their cross and follow the Lord Jesus.

If God has touched your heart on the powerful work of the cross, this is a good time to stop and thank him for the work done there. His intention is to set you free through his power unleashed at the cross. The work of the cross unleashes the divine power of God for salvation and brings defeat to God's enemy. May it be so in our experience.

The Word of God

"In the beginning was the Word..." **John 1:1**

We began this book by stating that words are powerful. Indeed, the purpose of every chapter has been to reveal the great power that lies beneath the surface of some of our most treasured Christian words. To close, we'll examine the most powerful word of all: the Word of God.

The Word of God is of incredible importance to those who follow Christ. The experience of many regarding the Word involves hearing a message from the Bible once a week and, for the truly committed, following that up with a daily reading based in the Scriptures. But God wants more than that. While those can be good, they do not represent our total relationship with the Word of God. Here are some New Testament aspects of the Word of God that may be missed or not fully considered:

The Word of God gives us light	John 1:4
The Word of God spreads	Acts 6:7
The Word of God makes us clean	Ephesians 5:26
The Word of God is mysterious	Colossians 1:26
The Word of God carries out God's work in you	I Thess. 2:13
The Word of God is sanctifying	I Timothy 4:5
The Word of God is freeing	II Timothy 2:9
The Word of God is active and discerning	Hebrews 4:12

The Word of God is edible	Hebrews 6:5
The Word of God is creative	Hebrews 11:3
The Word of God gives us life	I Peter 1:23
The Word of God is drinkable	I Peter 2:2
The Word of God abides in us	I John 2:14
The Word of God is God	John 1:1
The Word of God is Christ	John 1:14
The Word of God is the Spirit	Ephesians 6:17

This is not an exhaustive list, but it signals that the Word of God is very powerful. If you have need of any of the above, help is not far away; it's found by deepening your relationship with the Word of God.

God is a Communicator

God has always been a communicator. He began by speaking his creation into existence. *"Then God said..."* is the hallmark of each day's creative handiwork in Genesis 1. Moreover, there are close to 260 references in the Old Testament to the "Word of the Lord" being given to the Israelites. Yes, we have a speaking God. That makes an intimate relationship with the Word of God very relevant to us.

In most cases when we hear the expression "the Word of God," we instantly think of the written Scriptures. We are often encouraged to do such things as "spend time in the Word"; "study the Word"; and "memorize the Word." When the Word of God is used in this way, it obviously refers to the Bible. The word "Bible" is the English form of the Greek word *biblia*, which meant "books" and referred to the collection of Scriptures whose earliest copies date back to the second century. It was brought into English use by the translator John Wycliffe in the late 1300s. No doubt, those who are believers in Christ will agree that there is no other book like it. It is the divine record of redemption and God's love for mankind.

What's the best book you've read this month? A spy thriller, a romantic love story, a real-life drama about world events or something in the historical fiction category? Whatever it might be, chances are, once read, it will join all the other books on your bookshelf, rarely to be read again. Not so the Bible. This is a book that again and again, month after month, year after year, provides inspiration, refreshment, comfort and guidance. It is a book of light, life and freedom. Above all, the Bible invites us beyond its own pages and into the very fellowship of God the Father and his Son, Jesus Christ. As glorious as the Scriptures are, does the Word of God, in its fullness, incorporate more than the written words of God? The answer is a definite Yes.

The Word in Fullness

We can say with great confidence that Jesus Christ is the living Word of God. That in no way devalues the Scriptures. When the written Word is rightly understood, it leads us to the living Word and, through him, to real life.

If the written Word is handled wrongly, however, the result can be confusion, legalism and even condemnation. For many Christians, sadly, reading the Bible is an act of Christian duty carried out because they know it is necessary if they want to grow as believers. Because the Scriptures have often been applied in a legalistic way, they actually have been used as an instrument of pain rather than one of liberty. Many people are hesitant to admit that they more often find condemnation in the Bible's pages than encouragement and life. Perhaps you are in that category. If so, take heart. There are richer days ahead in your experience of the Word of God.

The best place to reclaim an understanding of the Word of God is in John's Gospel. *"In the beginning was the Word, and the Word was with God, and the Word was God. He was in the beginning with God. All things came into being through him, and apart from him nothing came into being that has come into being. In him was life, and the life was the Light of men"* (John 1:1-4). Consider the Word referred to in this passage. This Word predates time, was oriented toward God and, in fact, consisted of God himself. This Word was so full of creative life that the entire visible and invisible universe was made by him. When this Word spoke, light broke out like a million stars, dispelling utter darkness. This Word was there in Genesis 1 when the foundations of the heavens were laid, when the boundaries of the oceans were set, and when plant, animal and human kind were brought forth. This Word is awesome!!

This is our introduction to the Word of God: living, light-filled, creative and full of God. Would you like to have a deeper encounter with that Word? God made such an encounter possible. John 1:14 says *"And the Word became flesh, and dwelt among us, and we beheld his glory, glory as of the only begotten from the Father, full of grace and truth."* That living Word became a man whose name was Jesus. Jesus in human form was the expression of God the Father. He revealed to mankind what God was thinking. He brought the loving power of God to bear in the midst of a world in darkness. He still does so today. As the writer of Hebrews described the coming of Christ, *"God, after he spoke long ago to the fathers in the prophets in many portions and in many ways, in these last days has spoken to us in his Son, whom he appointed heir of all things, through whom also he made the world"* (Hebrews 1:1-2). Today God speaks to us in Jesus.

A War of Words

It can be fairly stated that in some measure the struggle between God and his enemy is a war of words. In the Garden of Eden, God instructed his man not to eat of the tree of the knowledge of good and evil. Satan showed up and twisted God's words. He started out his conversation with Eve by saying, *"Has God said…?"*

There's a lesson to be learned here: it's always dangerous to enter into conversation with the enemy of our souls.

You know how the story goes from there. In the war of twisted words, man was deceived and Satan won that battle. God's words were negated. It took the death of God's own Son to remedy the damage that resulted.

Let's watch how the living Word Jesus behaved when he encountered this same enemy in Matthew 4:1-4: *"Jesus was led up by the Spirit into the wilderness to be tempted by the devil. After he had fasted forty days and forty nights, he then became hungry. The tempter came and said to him, 'If you are the Son of God, command that these stones become bread.' But he answered and said, 'It is written, "Man shall not live on bread alone, but on every word that proceeds out of the mouth of God.""'* Is it not interesting that the weapons in this face-off were not swords but words, and in this confrontation, as in the Garden of Eden, the subject matter was food? Jesus was hungry and in a weakened state. The enemy probably thought it would be easy to tempt Jesus to follow his advice. But Jesus did not succumb. He had a higher food source than mere bread. His food source was the speaking of his Father within him. That speaking word told him to denounce the advance of the tempter. The implication is plain to see. Bread alone cannot give you life. In the broader spectrum, earthly things cannot satisfy you. You were designed to be nourished by the words of God. You were designed to draw sustenance by hearing from your heavenly Father. Without that heavenly guidance, you cannot fully live. Notice that Jesus answers the question as a man, rather than as the Son of God. This is important because if he as a man with God living in him can defeat the enemy by the word of God, then you and I as men and women with Christ living in us can defeat the same enemy in the same way.

Shortly afterward Jesus began his public ministry. Here's how he started: *"From that time Jesus began to preach and say, 'Repent, for the kingdom of heaven is at hand'"* (Matthew 4:17). The Word of God that Jesus declared let mankind know that the kingdom of heaven was available to men and women on planet earth. The Word of God makes known to us the resources of the heavens so that we, like Jesus, can live in heavenly realms and defeat God's enemy. Jesus was the living Word, and he knew the power that his words contained. He knew there was a revolutionary life force in them. That's why he said, *"Therefore everyone who hears these words of mine and acts upon them may be compared to a wise man who built his house on the rock."* (Matthew 7:24). When he spoke people were drawn to him, made aware of their need for God, healed and cleansed. As he said to his followers in John 15:3, *"You are already clean because of the word which I have spoken to you."* Do you need cleansing from the dirt that the world throws at you? Spend some time with the Lord Jesus. Allow him to wash you with his cleansing presence. That's what happens when we encounter the Word of God. As Jesus put it in John 14:23, *"If anyone loves me, he will keep my word; and my Father will love him, and we will come to him and make our abode with him."* Holding tight to the Word of God leads us into the love of God; into intimate fellowship with the Father and the Son. Such encounters with the Word change us profoundly.

The Word as Spirit

Those who met Jesus were amazed at the power and authority of his words. Consider these passages:

Luke 2:47: *"And all who heard him were amazed at his understanding and his answers."*

Luke 4:32: *"...and they were amazed at his teaching, for his message was with authority."*

Luke 4:36: *"And amazement came upon them all, and they began talking with one another saying, 'What is this message? For with authority and power he commands the unclean spirits and they come out.'"*

Luke 8:25: *"They were fearful and amazed, saying to one another, 'Who then is this that he commands even the winds and the water, and they obey him?'"*

It is obvious that Jesus spoke as no other. But what would happen to this powerful Word when Jesus was crucified, resurrected and ascended? What would happen when he was no longer physically present to carry out the thoughts and will of his Father? Jesus' plan was not to substitute his presence with talks about the kind of person he was, the rules that he left us to live by, and the good deeds we should do to help our fellow man until we see him again someday in heaven. There is more to the Word of God than that.

Here is what Jesus said to his followers in John 14:16: *"I will ask the Father, and he will give you another Helper, that he may be with you forever; that is the Spirit of truth, whom the world cannot receive, because it does not behold him or know him, but you know him because he abides with you and will be in you. I will not leave you as orphans; I will come to you."* Jesus Christ, the living Word, would return as the Spirit of Truth and so indwell his disciples.

Jesus clarified what the Spirit of Truth would do a few verses later: *"When the Helper comes, whom I will send to you from the Father, that is the Spirit of truth who proceeds from the Father, he will bear witness of Me, and you will bear witness also, because you have been with Me from the beginning"* (John 15:26). And a few verses later in chapter 16, v. 13, *"But when he, the Spirit of truth, comes, he will guide you into all the truth; for he will not speak on his own initiative, but whatever he hears, he will speak; and he will disclose to you what is to come. He will glorify Me, for he will take of mine and will disclose it to you…A little while, and you will no longer see Me; and again a little while, and you will see Me."* Testify; hear; speak; disclose; it sounds like this Spirit of Truth would be doing a lot of communicating.

Jesus, the Word in flesh, became the Word dwelling in us as Spirit. This Word glorifies Christ; he reveals the will of the Father and guides us into a living relationship with the Lord Jesus. This is the Word of God unleashed to do his creative work in us. Notice that the Spirit will testify of Christ and we will do the same. That's exactly what happened in the New Testament church. The Word of God is the testimony of Jesus Christ. That testimony did not stop with the heavenly ascension of Christ. Here's what happened in the book of Acts: *"And when they* [the disciples] *had prayed, the place where they had gathered together was shaken, and they were all filled with the Holy Spirit and began to speak the Word of God with boldness"* (Acts 4:31). That Word of God was God's message concerning his Son, Jesus Christ. As verse 33 says, *"with great power the apostles were giving witness to the resurrection of the Lord Jesus, and abundant grace was upon them all."*

The resurrected Lord, now living in his followers, continued to broadcast the Word of God. As Acts 6:7 records, *"The word of God kept on spreading; and the number of the disciples continued to increase greatly in Jerusalem."* But it wouldn't stop there. As Jesus said to his disciples before he ascended in Acts 1:8, *"but you shall receive power when the Holy Spirit has come upon you; and you shall be my witnesses both in Jerusalem, and in all Judea and Samaria, and even to the remotest part of the earth."* The

Word reached Samaria in Acts 8 when Philip went to preach there. As the Scriptures tell us, *"Therefore, those who had been scattered went about preaching the word. Philip went down to the city of Samaria and began proclaiming Christ to them"* (Acts 8:4-5). Do we see the connection? Preaching the word is proclaiming Christ and his kingdom. Verse 12 tells us that Philip's message was the good news of the kingdom of God and the Name of Jesus. In Acts 8:14 we read, *"Now when the apostles in Jerusalem heard that Samaria had received the word of God, they sent them Peter and John."* Through the ministry of Peter, John and, later on, Paul and others, this living Word would go out to the ends of the known world.

We see this in Acts 13 when God sent Paul and Barnabas out to take the good news to the nations. They started off on the island of Cyprus, where they preached in the Jewish synagogues. But the Jewish leaders turned against them and started speaking out against their message. Here was Paul's response: *"Paul and Barnabas spoke out boldly and said, 'It was necessary that the word of God be spoken to you first; since you repudiate it and judge yourselves unworthy of eternal life, behold, we are turning to the Gentiles'...When the Gentiles heard this, they began rejoicing and glorifying the word of the Lord; and as many as had been appointed to eternal life believed. And the word of the Lord was being spread through the whole region"* (Acts 13:46-49).

The Word in You

The powerful Word of God is spreading, growing, and producing eternal life in those who received Jesus Christ. The Word of the Lord results in salvation. The Word of the Lord brings glory to Jesus Christ. When God speaks, the heart is joyful. That Word went out into all the earth and one day reached you. If you received the Word, new life began. Peter described this process in his first letter: *"For you have been born again not of seed which is perishable but imperishable, that is, through the living and abiding word of God. for, 'All flesh is like grass, And all its glory like the flower of grass. The grass withers, and the flower falls off, But the word of the Lord endures forever.' And this is the word which was preached to you"* (I Peter 1:23-25).

Peter let us know that this Word was Christ when he wrote, *"like newborn babies, long for the pure milk of the word, so that by it you may grow in respect to salvation, if you have tasted the kindness of the Lord. And coming to him as to a living stone which has been rejected by men, but is choice and precious in the sight of God, you also, as living stones, are being built up as a spiritual house for a holy priesthood, to offer up spiritual sacrifices acceptable to God through Jesus Christ"* (I Peter 2: 1-5).

If you are a believer, the Living Word of God, one with the Father, active in creation, made flesh, crucified, buried and resurrected, now lives in you. You can go to him for drink, for food, for fellowship, and to be built together with others into the house of God. No wonder Paul wrote to the believers in Colosse, *"Let the word of Christ richly dwell within you, with all wisdom teaching and admonishing one another with psalms and hymns and spiritual songs, singing with thankfulness in your hearts to God"* (Colossians 3:16). As we open the door of our hearts to this living Word, he gives us what we need to enrich the body of Christ.

Paul wrote the same thing to those in Ephesus when he said, *"For this reason I bow my knees before the Father...that he would grant you, according to the riches of his glory, to be strengthened with power through his Spirit in the inner man, so that Christ may dwell in your hearts through faith; and that you, being rooted and grounded in love, may be able to comprehend with all the saints what is the breadth and length and height and depth, and to know the love of Christ which surpasses knowledge, that you may be filled up to all the fullness of God"* (Ephesians 3:14-19). Christ, the living Word of God, surrounds us with the love of God and fills us up with the fullness of God. That's a powerful Word.

This is exactly what Paul had in mind when he wrote, *"Of this I was made a minister according to the stewardship from God bestowed on me for your benefit, so that I might make full the word of God"* (Colossians 1:25). Paul had just finished describing how full the Word of God is in the preceding verses when he wrote, *"For by him all things were created, both in the heavens and on earth, visible and invisible...all things have been created through him and for him. He is before all things, and in him all things hold together."* Is Paul speaking here of the Word or of Christ? Both! The two are one. Paul goes on, *"he is also head of the body, the church; and he is the beginning, the firstborn from the dead, so that he himself will come to have first place in everything, for it was the Father's good pleasure for all the fullness to dwell in him."* That is Christ in his Body, the Word of God made full. The amazing thing is that we are a part of this fullness. You and I have been made part of that body, the fullness of him who fills all in all.

The Word Allows Us to Rest

The good news is that the less we do in our own power, the more the Lord accomplishes in us. When it comes to the Word of God, our job is to find our rest in him and allow the Word to do its creative work. This is what the writer of Hebrews told Jewish believers scattered across the first century world: *"There remains therefore a Sabbath rest for the people of God. For the one who has entered his rest has himself also rested from his works, as God did from his. Let us therefore be diligent to enter that rest, lest anyone fall, through following the same example of disobedience"* (Hebrews 4:9). The Old Testament disobedience that the writer referred to was ignoring the Word of God. They failed to believe that what God was telling them was true.

In the New Testament, Christ is presented to us as the Word of God. He is the one who gives us rest. He is the one who satisfies the requirements of the law in us. He is the one who communicates to us the love, mercy and grace of God. He is the one who takes us out of death and into life. That's why this passage continues with these well known words, *"For the word of God is living and active and sharper than any two-edged sword, and piercing as far as the division of soul and spirit, of both joints and marrow, and able to judge the thoughts and intentions of the heart. And there is no creature hidden from his sight, but all things are open and laid bare to the eyes of him with whom we have to do. Since then we have a great high priest who has passed through the heavens, Jesus the Son of God, let us hold fast our confession"* (Hebrews 4:12-14).

While these verses are often used to refer to the Bible, a closer look reveals that they refer to the Lord Jesus, himself. He is the Word of God, living in us as Spirit and actively carrying out the Father's will in us. He is the one who knows better than we do what is in our hearts, and he is the one who is able to guide us into the truth. Note the wording of verse 14: *"there is no creature* **hidden from**

his sight, *but all things are open and laid bare* **to the eyes of him** *with whom we have to do."* These verses refer back to the Word of God, a person before whom we are totally exposed and who is actively interested in who we are and what we are doing. That person is the Lord Jesus. He knows who you are. He knows what you need. He knows where you fall short. Go to him and allow him to speak peace, joy, love and life into your life. Often he will use the words of Scripture to communicate those things to you. They are a powerful tool in his hands.

As we learn to rest in Christ and allow him to do his work in us, the creative power of the Word of God is unleashed in our lives. That's why a following verse encourages us to *"draw near with confidence to the throne of grace, so that we may receive mercy and find grace to help in time of need,"* (Verse 16). Thank God, his Word is full of mercy and grace—just what we need to follow a holy and living Lord. Will it be boring? No! That life of resting in Christ kicks off a whole new level of spiritual activity in our walk with him and in fellowship with his body.

The Sword of the Spirit

In Ephesians 6 Paul shows us what that spiritual activity will look like. He encouraged the believers to take up the whole armor of God and in that armor to stand. He reminded them that we do not struggle with flesh and blood but with the principalities and powers of darkness in heavenly places. He conceded that there is wrestling involved but declared we will be able to stand firm, that we will be able to resist and *"extinguish all the flaming arrows of the evil one."* This is our heritage in Jesus Christ. He won the victory over Satan and lives to make that victory real for us.

While we learn to rest in Christ, as God's people we are called to do battle with God's enemy. According to Ephesians 6, we are clothed with truth, protected by righteousness, shielded by faith, covered with salvation and standing in peace. All of these are aspects of what the Lord Jesus is to us. He is the truth (John 14:6); he is our righteousness (I Corinthians 1:30); he is the source of our faith (I Timothy 1:14); he is our peace (Ephesians 2:14) and our salvation (Hebrews 5:9). These are all awesome attributes that we can rejoice in as followers of Christ. But what do we need when we are to go out and take the battle to the enemy? What is it that will drive the enemy to his knees and lead to his ultimate destruction? For that we will need a mighty weapon. That weapon is the Word of God.

Here is what Paul said: *"And take...the sword of the Spirit, which is the Word of God."* Please note, the Spirit does not wave a sword. The Spirit is a sword. That sword is called the Word of God. The Word of God, the Lord Jesus, active in creation, made visible in flesh, now in Spirit, is our weapon in storming the gates of hell. What better armament could we ask for? Remember the description of the Word of God in Hebrews 4: living, active, sharper than any two-edged sword, able to discern the thoughts and intents of the heart, and keenly aware of what is going on in your life. This is your Jesus, the Word that you are to turn to and rest in as you move forward in the kingdom work that God has called you to.

It's helpful to realize that this is a corporate calling and we are individually part of it. This battle takes an army. As important as each of us is, no one of us can put on all that God is. We are called to be part of Christ's body. That is where we find the fullness of him who fills all in all. We need our brothers and sisters in Christ to stand with us in this mighty calling. Paul knew that. That's why he ended this section with these words: *"With all prayer and petition pray at all times in the Spirit, and with this in view, be on the alert with all perseverance and petition for all the saints, and pray on my behalf, that utterance may be given to me in the opening of my mouth, to make known with boldness the mystery of the gospel"* (Ephesians 6:18-19). The Ephesians were encouraged to go to Christ in their spirits and, energized by him, pray for one another and for Paul as he continued to make known the good news of Christ. This is how the word of God spreads and grows. May it be so in our midst.

We are all familiar with the saying "a picture is worth a thousand words." But that is not true when it comes to the Lord Jesus. Better we should say this Word can launch a thousand pictures. The fact is that pictures themselves are dependent on words to make them come descriptively alive. Words have the power to draw us in a way that pictures, smells and sounds can't. That is true of the Word of God. God draws the unsaved to him by his Word. Then, through his Word, he draws those who are saved to an ever-closer walk with him. If you have been drawn closer to God through anything written in this book, I hope you will respond by inviting the Lord to take you into a closer relationship with him.

A Final Look

In closing this chapter, it's fitting to take one last look at Jesus Christ. He is our Captain, the One who has formed us, died for us, called us and never forsakes us. Here is how the apostle John described him in Revelation 19:11-13: *"And I saw heaven opened, and behold, a white horse, and he who sat on it is called Faithful and True, and in righteousness he judges and wages war. His eyes are a flame of fire, and on his head are many diadems; and he has a name written on him which no one knows except himself. He is clothed with a robe dipped in blood, and his name is called The Word of God."*

The One whose robe is dipped in blood and whose name is The Word of God is riding out to make the kingdom of his Father a visible and eternal reality. He is calling you. Will you ride with him? You have been cleansed by his blood. You have been born again by the living Word. Now allow the living Word who is Christ to dwell in you richly. He will bring the reality and love of the Father to bear in your life. Ask him to put you in the company of others who have a heart to know him. He will hear and answer those prayers. In the meantime we can say to him with anticipation…

Yes, Lord, we will ride with you.

Epilogue

Light vs. Knowledge

"And God said, Let there be light: and there was light." **Genesis 1: 3**

Do you remember when God first became real to you? I remember it well. My first sense was that the lights had been turned on. For the first time I could see how my life fit into God's design for his creation. Everything made sense. My hope in writing this book is that the light of God will shine brighter from the words that are central to our experience as believers, that they will make more sense to you. As you go forward in your walk with the Lord, I pray that the light that you have seen in these chapters will show the way to a deeper experience with him.

But there's a caution flag ahead. We must guard the light that God has given.

Across the bay from my home town of San Francisco sits Berkeley, California, home to a major university campus. In the middle of the Berkeley campus is a large clock tower called the Campanile. Its profile dominates the Berkeley skyline. On top of that tower is inscribed a portion of the verse cited above: "Let there be light."

But these words do not refer to the same glorious light that God initiates in Genesis 1. They do not refer to the clarity that we receive when we understand the world from God's perspective.

What is being elevated on that tower is knowledge—the knowledge that comes from sitting in classrooms and listening to professors interpret history, philosophy, science and other areas of study. In the minds of most educators, light is equated with knowledge. We have the perception that the knowledge a person receives by going to a university and sitting at the feet of the professors enables him or her to live a fully developed life. Is that knowledge bad or of little use? In most cases not. But as a graduate of that same University of California system, I can tell you the knowledge most often presented is devoid of the light that reveals how God is working in this universe.

An experience one of my sons had in college reflects this. One of his professors opened the fall session by saying, "I used to be a Catholic, but don't worry; now I'm an atheist." As an atheist, he was quite sure what he had to teach would be of more relevance than something presented by a believer in God. The exclusion of God from college classrooms in our time is the rule, not the exception.

When God said, "Let there be light," he was talking about a light of a totally different nature. It wasn't the sun, because the sun hadn't been created yet. That happened on the fourth day of creation. On the first day light banished darkness and created an anticipation of good things to come. This light revealed that God was about to do something. And thank God, he did!

What's the first thing you would do if you were about to work in a dark place? Sure, you'd turn on the light. And that's what God did. He wanted to work in the darkness of the physical world and so he turned on the light. Today, he wants to work in your life so he starts by turning on the light of Jesus Christ.

But let's be clear: light and knowledge are not equivalent. In God's vocabulary, light contains knowledge but it is much more than that. This light is the radiance of God's glory and presence. On day one of creation, God allowed his radiance to visibly illuminate an earth in darkness. His light works the same way today, casting the light of the glory of Christ into our spiritual darkness. As the apostle Paul wrote, *"For God, who said Light shall shine out of darkness, is the One who has shone in our hearts, to give the light of the knowledge of the glory of God in the face of Christ"* (II Corinthians 4:6).

If this greater light, then, is important to God, his enemy will do what he can to minimize its impact. We believers must not allow that to happen.

Consider this: the so-called "enlightened ones" in our society have become the intellectuals, the well educated, and the artists. They are certainly not those who hold a simple faith in the Lord Jesus. In most cases, where are these "enlightened ones" leading us? It's not into a greater realization and experience of the loving God who created all things. The greater the impact of our so called "enlightened" community, seemingly the lower our standards of morality sink. While there are educators and artists working to increase righteousness in our land, there's little doubt that the majority voice seeks to draw us away from rather than toward God.

It's not just in America where this happens. The enlightened ones in India, for example, are the gurus, who leave their families and all material possessions to live lives of complete denial. Many of them walk naked through the streets. I have seen them covering themselves with dirt and wearing long tails to honor the monkey god. I have seen them bowing down and making offerings before seven-headed golden cobras on behalf of fearful masses. They are the enlightened ones.

Is that true light? No.

And what about the so-called "Age of Enlightenment?" Was that a period of history where the knowledge of the true God and his desire for mankind was heralded around the world? The hallmark of the Age of Enlightenment was not God but Reason. Reason did not lead that era to God. That is what light is for.

Light opens the door to life. And life is found in Christ.

When Jesus Christ came to earth, the apostle John described him as follows: *"In him was life, and the life was the light of men."* In Luke, Zacharias the priest described Jesus as one who would *"give light to them that sit in darkness and in the shadow of death, to guide our feet into the way of peace."* Also in Luke 2:30, when the infant Jesus was presented

157

for dedication, the prophet Simeon declared, *"My eyes have seen your salvation, which you prepared for all peoples, a light to the Gentiles and the glory of your people Israel."* Jesus himself declared to his followers in John 8:12, *"I am the light of the world: he that follows me shall not walk in darkness, but shall have the light of life."*

We can see from these verses that real light is something far more than knowledge. Real light is the presence of Christ himself, who is the image and radiance of God. He is the One who illuminates the path for us, showing us how to know God and follow him.

Jesus Christ came to turn the light on in our lives. It's time to say to him, "Lord, turn on the light. Reveal who you are and what your purposes are." The purpose of this book is not to increase your knowledge. Rather, it is to shine light on the centrality and greatness of Christ through focusing on great words that he has given us. Friends, follow the light into a deeper life with Christ.

Resist the inclination to be a knowledge seeker. Instead, become one who sits in the presence of Christ and allows him to illuminate your world. The result will be life, real life. Don't rush to simply pack truth into your head. Ask the Lord to give you light on some aspect of his love for you or to speak to you about something that he wishes to do. If he has spoken to you through the words of this book, invite him to work their meaning deep into your experience. God said, "Let there be light…and there was." It is his intention to shine light into our lives. He will answer your prayer.

Finally, this book is bait. It is thrown out into the vast ocean that is modern-day Christendom to lure hungry believers into a richer experience with their Lord. There is far more to our glorious Lord than any book could capture or any one person's experience could contain. But if your appetite has been whetted and you have been drawn into a more intimate relationship with your Lord, contact us at Hope Builders International, P.O. Box 317, Greenwood, VA 22943 and share your story with us. Let your light loose. As God is unleashed in the lives of men and women, his kingdom expands. Recapturing our Christian vocabulary and unleashing the divine activity of God in our lives can only serve to draw us closer to him and make his purposes our purposes. May it be so, Lord Jesus.